The Likeness

PETER LANG
New York • Washington, D.C./Baltimore • Boston • Bern
Frankfurt am Main • Berlin • Brussels • Vienna • Canterbury

María-Xosé Queizán

The Likeness

Translated from the Galician language by
Ana M. Spitzmesser

PETER LANG
New York • Washington, D.C./Baltimore • Boston • Bern
Frankfurt am Main • Berlin • Brussels • Vienna • Canterbury

Library of Congress Cataloging-in-Publication Data

Queizán, María-Xosé.
[Semellanza. English]
The likeness / María-Xosé Queizán; translated by Ana M. Spitzmesser.
p. cm.
Includes bibliographical references.
1. Spitzmesser, Ana María. II. Title.
PQ9469.2.Q4A62913   869.3'42—dc21   98-32075
ISBN 0-8204-4177-5

Die Deutsche Bibliothek-CIP-Einheitsaufnahme

Queizán, María-Xosé:
The likeness / María-Xosé Queizán. Transl. by Ana M. Spitzmesser.
–New York; Washington, D.C./Baltimore; Boston; Bern;
Frankfurt am Main; Berlin; Brussels; Vienna; Canterbury Paris: Lang.
ISBN 0-8204-4177-5

Cover design by Nona Reuter

Originally published in the Galician language as *A semellanza*
Permission for this edition was arranged through Sotelo Blanco Edicións, S.L.
Santiago de Compostela, Galice.

The paper in this book meets the guidelines for permanence and durability
of the Committee on Production Guidelines for Book Longevity
of the Council of Library Resources.

∞

Printed in the United States of America

Don't laugh; it's a sad story

Castelao

The similar is known by its similarity

Empedocles

Table of Contents

Chapter 1

With light fingers, she rearranges the tie clasp, a gold cloisonné ruby she remembered in her grandfather's shirt front, and gives a final touch to the dazzling white handkerchief with the hand embroidered initials "CV" emerging from the jacket's upper pocket in a perfect peak. She would have liked her husband to wear a tie-knot in order to make it herself, just as Mama used to do for Papa, but she realized that nowadays ties were more modern; more functional.

After lunch, and as a part of their daily ritual, Merceditas went with her husband into the hall. There she inspected him from head to toe to verify that his black shoes were shiny, his cuffs starched and immaculate, and not even a speck of dust marred the perfectly cut tambourine suit. The inspection finished, she kissed him engagingly, pleased with the way he looked. It was for this, for his appearance alone, that she had married him, overlooking his lack of imagination and the absence of lively expression.

She calculated the time it would take him to get down the stairs with his ceremonial gait, which seemed as if a pavane was perennially playing in his ear. Lifting slightly one corner of the lace curtain of the living room window she watched him cross the street, once more admiring his figure, the elegance of his movements, the pull of the nonchalant cane he carried, like Celso Viéitez did, as an ornament. That day it was ebony, with a silver handle representing a panther's head.

Finally she saw him turn the street corner. It was a clear summer afternoon, but soon, with the arrival of autumn, mist and fog would come down blurring the bones and chilling the thoughts. In the dark days of winter, she could hardly make out her husband even in that stretch of the street. But nevertheless she could follow the balanced rhythm of his steps, the brief stop at the street's corner to change directions, the slight inclination of his erect head, the melancholy bright gaze of his black eyes. Celso Viéitez then became a knight of the mist. He could be idolized by his wife, and even seen at a par with those ancestors, misted for years and centuries, that filled Merceditas' mind. How handsome her husband was! Merceditas could not have borne to go out on the street on the arm of a country bumpkin, a jerk or one of those oafs like Nazario Abel, to mention one, who no doubt was a great man, as the fame of the city's chorale glorious music proved, but the way he walked, St. Xil! The opposite of her own husband, so straight. So distinguished!

Celso Viéitez, Merceditas' adored husband, went on as usually to the tertulia of the Artistic Club where the important men of the city reviewed the daily events, either as published on the daily newspaper or bandied about by gossip, while imbibing coffee and brandy. The tertulia was nicknamed "The syphon," and was well known as one of the most ingenious and corrosive coteries of the town. The serious and solemn Celso Viéitez was ill-equipped to compete with its steely-tongued members. One of them was don Lino, a great tease and a tale bearer, who at night would also grace the Méndez's tertulia to obtain more tidbits. Of don Lino it could be said that he would even notice the grass growing on city walls. Nothing that happened in the region or in the country escaped his keen eyes. His conversation would shift adroitly from the concrete to the abstract. He was not a simple gossip; his curiosity reached all cultural themes and spaces. He spoke several languages. He was familiar with general history and the recent intrahistory of the country, having met personally many of its participants. Don Lino's encyclopedic knowledge and many fields of interest attracted him a wide audience: civil servants, teachers, artists and such who, for different reasons, joined him for coffee and drinks with unfailing regularity.

When Celso Viéitez arrived at the Club, conversation was swirling around Xulia Minguillón, of whom *O Progreso* was announcing a new painting exhibition. As usual, she was inevitably measured up against Maruja Mallo, another woman painter from Lugo. Mallo's grays versus Minguillón's street scenes—and from here a discussion on avant-garde painters ensued. The political debate was served with Arab-Jewish relations in Palestine. According to the local newspapers, England was willing to build a federated Palestinian state, thus achieving peace and harmony between both parties, all of course with the support of the United States of America.

"I doubt very much they can pull it off. Both sides have their own right to claim the territory for themselves," said don Angel after tasting his drink.

"It must be terrible for the Jews, I mean, being without a country," said Cesáreo Corbal spilling ash from the cigar he was smoking over his voluminous paunch, and not bothering to remove it.

That Cesáreo, used to say Merceditas to her husband when they saw him on the street, poor man, he is really broke.

"That is not new. Even in Roman times, the Jews were expelled from the place. The situation is as old as our city walls," pointed out knowingly a history professor at the local university.

"I'd say it is like a curse, always scattered over the world, I mean, always wandering...Like in the zarzuela—" observed Cesáreo animatedly, letting his coffee spill over his shirt due to the motion of his hand holding the cup—"You know, what? *The Wandering Jew*"—and he starts humming with his old tenor voice.

Don Cesáreo did not miss any opportunity to lead the conversation towards music topics in which he was an expert. After this, he probably went on to the *Trovador*, remembering well Hipólito Lázaro on the occasion he sang in Lugo during the last opera season, at least twenty years before, I mean, how time flies—.

"We are no less wandering people," cut in Trapero before Cesáreo's musical impulses were given full rein. "People from Galicia can be found in every sea, every port, every hole in the world."

"I mean—"said Cesáreo with a voice hoarse from the effort of letting himself being heard.

"Here, drink up. You sound like a Santalices hornpipe,"–said don Angel offering him a glass.

"But it isn't the same. I mean, we have our own country," he drinks unwillingly, and some water also spills over his stomach. "Even if it is just to be buried in, all of them come back here."

"We plow over the dead in this land, and our bread has the taste of our family bodies, brothers," quoted don Lino ponderously.

"Say, man, what's that"? everybody asked.

"It's a magnificent sonnet dedicated to Rey–Xordo, a leader of the Irmandiños. It was written by Lorenzo Varela."

"That name sounds familiar. I mean—"

"Of course, silly. He went to school with us. He lives in Argentina now. You see? A wandering Galego. We also have those. And not all of them can return," said don Lino.

"He is an exile? I mean, one of those rebels"?

"A Communist," answered don Lino lowering his voice.

"Well, it is a fact that Galegos are everywhere doing everything. It is as if distance would increase their wits. Everything. When I was a boy, Monsieur Blondin, the world famous tightrope walker, I don't know if you remember, the one who crossed over Niagara Falls, came to Lugo. It was quite a stir. Phenomenal! He was to cross the Plaza Mayor from end to end, and the whole town was there holding their breath. Seeing those great heights I told a friend: 'What a fright! He is going to crash!' And Monsieur Blondin himself, who happened just to go by us at that moment, said to me: 'Fie! fie!' while making the fig with his fingers. He was from Ourense!"

Manolo Figueroa came along at that moment, apologizing for the delay. He had been nominated recently "Companion of the Syphon," and he brought the news of a proposed excursion to the Oseira monastery. On this occasion the group's password would be: 'We don't believe even in the sea level.' He was enthusiastically received by those present.

"How come you are so late, man?"

"Don't' ask. On my way over I saw Anton de Marcos taking care of Luis Pimentel who was sitting on a bench in the plaza complaining that he was dying, that he was losing consciousness, that his heart was stopping—Anton, white as a sheet, all panicky, you know him, thinking that the man was about to die—."

"He is a simpleton to take him seriously."

"That man Pimentel, always the same," said don Lino as if discussing some childish prank. "He has made a hole in his wrist by checking his pulse so often with fear that his heart will stop." He laughed haltingly. "But nothing doing, it's just nerves."

"One of these days he will really die of it," said Celso.

"Sure. Just like all of us," replied don Lino.

"He is a hypochondriac, that's all."

"A hypo—what? I mean—"

"He acts that way for lack of anything better to do," said Figueroa.

"Yes, like all of us," said don Lino closing down the argument.

Nobody had anything else to say.

While her husband was at the tertulia, Merceditas was enjoying a quiet moment of placidity and solitude dozing in the half shadow of her small sitting room, abandoning herself to the daydreams and memories of her childhood at the family manor. She was alone. Shortly after his father, her little boy had gone out with the nanny that took him to the park to play. The house was silent, open to foolishness. Nothing could interrupt the unraveling of Merceditas' nostalgic fantasies.

The guitar shaped grandfather clock, with its big, heavy weights, stroke half past the hour. The wooden box was rather moth-eaten since it was well over a hundred years old. It had come from great-grandfather's house down by the Mera river. When she was a child she had heard that during a notorious water rise, the clock and other furniture pieces had ended up in the river. Miraculously, the clock was not swallowed up by the current, reappearing several days later in the eddies by the Corgo bridge, entwined with a big bread bin. In Merceditas opinion, the muffled chiming sound, ton, ton, already slow, was due to all that wetness, like a chronic cold. Even thus, she preferred it to the sharp and silvery tin, tin of the oval clock in the dining room. The old, asthmatic clock was one of the pieces she liked best, the more perhaps because it brought a jumble of memories to her head rather than for its own rugged beauty. She attributed to it the loyalty of an old retainer who had refused to part from the family, fighting off the brute force of the river. It also reminded her of that figure of Christ worshipped in the seaside town of her birth; the one that, during the Napoleonic wars and according to believers, had refused to follow the marauding French invaders. After making the ship capsize, He had returned, not swimming Merceditas supposed, but ordering the waves to bring Him back to the beach where the original parish stood, in order to continue to protect them all, up there from his high altar.

On top of the rich dark woodside table with its beautifully carved legs, and resting on an embroidered Camariñas lace cloth, stood a Czech porcelain soup tureen with blue geometric pattern design. The tureen was the only piece left from the old family china. It made her remember the big dinner parties at home when she was a little girl. Her First Communion, Christmas, St. John's, grandfather's name day...Each piece broken by the kitchen servants was a source of great vexation for Mama. When too many pieces were gone they started to use the dishes every day. They bought a flower patterned set for "occasions," but she never cared for it. The tureen was salvaged by Merceditas. Its lid was cracked on one side, and when entering the room every day, the first thing she did was to see that the broken part was ensconced artfully against the wall, where nobody could notice. The maids were usually careless and placed it every which way.

Through the tureen, Merceditas could relive the big dinners of her childhood, presided over by her white bearded grandfather, with his shapely hands, always so refined and exquisite. She unfailingly saw him tall and majestic, which he was not; but perhaps this was because his slim figure, and his well-proportioned limbs made him look taller. He never grew a paunch, unlike so many other men his age. He enjoyed his food, but he was a gourmet rather than gourmand. Grandmother personally cooked his favorite dishes: baked turbot with bay leaves; rabbit cacciatore marinated the day before; vegetable stew with tender potatoes and fine herbs; conger empanada with roast peppers...It was dramatic to watch grandmother Otilia at work with her precise, rhythmic gestures. One could feel the pounding of the kneaded dough over the floured marble top, and grandmother's plump white arms going up and down, buttering up the dough again and again. Besides she was allowed to eat off the kitchen pans which, as a little girl, she preferred over any food on her plate. The greasy honey-colored leftovers she scraped out of the bottom with a silver teaspoon were a greater pleasure to her palate than the best morsels she would taste years later. Since the lard pickings were too heavy, she could not eat afterwards, and her mother had them banned. But with the complicity of Saladina, the kitchen maid, she could still revel in the forbidden pleasure. In secret, she also used to eat the cheese rinds left on dessert plates. She used to escape with them to the ironing closet where, kneeling over a stool that served as table, she could enjoy the smelly scraps to her heart's content.

How many things one could remember through the tureen! Many faces came to memory. Saladina, the maid, was already at the house when she was born. She had been brought almost a child from a tiny hamlet in the mountains. From time to time she got so homesick that she had to go back to her family for a while. During the first days upon her return, big tears would run down her cheeks, tears that would collect in the folds of her skin like small puddles. Saladina's face was scarred with smallpox. She was sick for her home. A woman without a home to live and die in was like a wind scattered leaf, she said. On the contrary, looking out the window of her humble dwelling, she could see herself as a little girl, taking the cows to pasture, or going to school. Such a long walk every day, clad in the woollen hood that her mother had knitted for her, and which proved a scant protection against winter colds. When Saladina relived her childhood days, even the smell of manure seemed a pleasant perfume to her. Here, in the town, Saladina complained, no one can ever smell anything.

Perhaps, because of Saladina's loyalty to her own surroundings, Merceditas was inclined to reminisce since childhood. She had come to profess a scorn of inconsequence, of rootlessness. Now that she herself was away from the places of her childhood, memories became her *leitmotiv*. Just to please her, her husband investigated the Valladares family lineage, and her ancestors became alive in her eyes, a part of everyday life.

The mantelpiece showed several family photographs. First her own wedding. Herself, both bold and demure under the flower crown, holding the countless meters of her tulle train. In her hands, she carried her orange blossom bouquet, from which long flower garlands and silk ribbons cascaded. The bouquet was almost as big as herself. Next to her, her husband, ramrod straight, impeccable as usual, holding in his hand a pair of gloves, white as his shirtfront. Next to his minuscule bow tie the handkerchief emerged from the top pocket close to the tuberose, please gentleman buy a tuberose, in his lapel. When looking at the old pictures, Merceditas always found them all a little overdressed. Her excessively long veil, the bouquet that came down to her feet, even the bow in her hair in the family picture when she was a little girl...An enormous bow in her head, another in the hips, forming a kind of girdle. What a extravagance! On the other hand, the parents, how austere they seemed, sitting straight, ready for the portrait and staring fixedly at the camera. Grandmama was wearing the French enamel pendentif round her neck; Grandpapa, showing off his handlebar mustache which could not harden his soft features or his perfect countenance. Another portrait showed the great–grandparents with their offspring, three long tressed girls in striped flouncing dresses and white stockings, and a boy, a little man in black shorts and also a striped shirt. Of the girls, two had died young, the poor angels, one of smallpox, the other of typhus. There was only one left, Otilia, her grandmother, to all effects an only child, since her brother, Uncle Ramón was as if he had never existed. Merceditas remembered him as a shadow, a kind of appearing and disappearing ghost around the big house, never bothering anyone. There was a time when she had been scared of him, though. It was when someone had made her fear the bogey man, a monster lurking in the village, they said, carrying a big sack (they also called him 'the sack man') and abducting little girls. At that time she would be horribly afraid of the pazo's corridors, where Uncle Ramón would appear around any corner, unexpected and mysterious as usual. That's the way he went around, silent and quiet like. Nobody paid him any attention. Grandfather had told her once that Uncle was just a little "peculiar." Even as an old man he always dressed nattily. He always wore soft colored print scarves round his neck madeing his face even more diffuse. He had quit school when he was twelve, and little by little withdrew into himself till he hardly spoke with anyone. He never had a girlfriend. He never worked. He passed his time in long walks, reading romantic poetry or concocting herbal and fruit liqueurs of various colors: green, red or yellow, which were later on displayed in bottles on the sideboard. Here, have a spot of this raspberry liqueur made by Ramón, Otilia would offer to visitors. Uncle Ramón never touched the stuff himself. He was a little "peculiar." As a child, Merceditas never understood the gestures made by the servants when uncle Ramón, wrapped in a flowered apron, went into the kitchen to minister to his liqueurs. What mystery did he hide? Now she was sorry that she never tried to talk to him, to discover some part of that hidden world. For she knew now that behind Uncle Ramón there was a secret, maybe a frustration, some kind of denial. But at that time all seemed normal to her. Nobody cared about his strange behavior; they were used to it. In the big house, under its daily routine, uncle Ramón didn't bother anyone. Merceditas thought that here, in the city, living in smaller houses, with hardly any servants—uncle Ramón would be a real problem to have around.

One of the portraits she loved to gaze at was her mother's. Taken in the pazo's sundeck the day of her coming out party, it showed her dressed in trailing white satin, with bell skirts, a small waist, and a yoke of chantilly lace ornated with small rhinestone buttons. Encased in a long lace glove, one of her arms rested upon a small white sable cape draped around the back of a rocking chair. Also she was captivated by a picture of grandmother Otilia with that handsome beau with the blond, waxed mustache she had fallen madly in love with. With the strength common to the women of the family, she had determined to have him or no one else. When the parents made enquiries about the young man's background, they were horrified to learn that he came from a tiny hamlet, the son of the local schoolteacher, and that he had not gone beyond the first year despite three terms at the University of Santiago. He seemed to pass his time dancing the quadrille in the casino with great success, spurning the study of the law in which his parents expected him to excel till he became at least a supreme court magistrate. The family savings were about exhausted when he met Otilia, Merceditas grandmother. The old hidalgo, Otilia's father, fumed:

"He is a nobody and a wastrel! Our Otilia could aspire to a great marriage if she wanted to. To mention just one, there is the son of—"

"I know about it," replied his wife, "but, what do you want? She is crazy about that young man. And I am not surprised—he is so handsome, and cuts such a figure,!" said the lady, rolling her eyes.

Great-grandfather knew there was nothing he could do. When it came to beauty, the women of his family were adamant. To be good looking, dress well, have an attractive smile—those were mandatory qualities to get into the good graces of such discerning women.

At that time landed property could still provide for certain luxuries. Just as if they were giving her a new pony to ride around the pazo, the parents agreed to the marriage of their daughter to the handsome stud who would contribute to the improvement of the Valladares progeny.

As the new depositary of their gentility, and of the exquisite family taste, Merceditas followed suit in her selection of a mate. But the family fortune was now in no condition to satisfy the aesthetic whims of its women. The war had spoiled too many lives. For Merceditas' chosen one the family were just able to secure, through bribery of course, a job with the Lugo City Council. It meant that the couple would have to settle down in town, coming to the pazo only for the holidays.

The tertulia over, its laziest members were doing their customary turn around the Roman wall encircling the city, which could be symbolic of the permanent siege they laid upon the town in the course of their daily conversation.

Like a stone ring that had wedded the city, the wall gave her substance. It had marked her historically as the guarded oppidum of the Romans, the Lucus Augusti, the capital of north Gallaecia at the time when she was just another Roman province. Paradoxically, it was the French who, at the time the city was in their hands, had used the wall for the purpose it was originally built, that is, as a war fortress. They barricaded themselves behind the ramparts to withstand the attack from the troops of the marquis of La Romana—the name being a fortuitous coincidence—who had come to reconquer the city as his own, as if belonging to his ancestors. People used to say that the wall had been erected to protect its builders from the freezing winter winds blowing over the city, the highest in Galicia, or perhaps to emphasize the power she withheld as capital of the Roman Gallaecia, and later on of the old Galician kingdom of medieval times.

Very little of the former splendor was left in impoverished post–civil war Lugo. Like a sick person that has lost her color but whose plump cheeks are still visible, the city preserved the dejected, partly crumbling walls as a memento of her mythical past.

Rather than a myth, for today's inhabitants the wall was a customary place to stroll around, a liberation from urban stuffiness, and a place where their horizons expanded to encompass the surrounding valleys, and the vast spaces visible from there.

From the wall, the grey pavement, the city's environmental grey portrayed by the painters, became a vast range of rolling greens that, bathed by the Miño and its tributaries, descended all the way from the faraway mountains to the valley. The Miño, still young and frisky, lies in silent fealty at the foot of the city. Like a handsome page paying homage to his lord but without daring to enter his castle, its waters will never invade the city, but they can envelop her in fogs arising from the river like frankincense. Thus it would seem, were it not for their piercing effect in the bones of the suffering Lucenses. After having paid its respects to the city, the Miño goes on to the longed for A Guardia where it will meet the sea. From the wall the river can be seen rolling by, a silver knight, watering the greening trees of its banks, the verdant meadows, the yellow green vegetables patches yonder, the dark green of the oak woods, the light green of the coppices, the verdigris of the cold birchtrees, and the blue green of the mountains receding in the distance.

The soft open space rested serene under the onlookers eyes, which were able to drift from the wide country expanse on one side, to the steel gray houses of the city on the other.

'Lugo of steel and honey' had sung a poet. On the down side, the vast view became a wilderness of dark huts, propped up on the oozing walls, and huddling miserably against the slippery cobbles like a worn out army. From the stone roofs of these ill looking dwellings, the original chimney stacks could still be glimpsed, torn down and crumbling, as mute traces of its past splendor. It was necessary to imagine them all, one by one, in their former power. They were within reach of the inquisitive walkers who could easily touch them if they wished to do so.

Suitable to their peasant origins, present–day tenants tended their gardens which stretched out in the open like pieces of green fabric lying amidst the flooded walls. The dirty patches where they grew cabbages were trampled about by the domestic pig, fattened to be eaten along with them. The soft wind wafted the scent of wild berries and live oak from the high mountains. It also carried the stench of obnoxious fumes reeking of chimney smoke, which in turn would blend into the mist perennially hanging over the city.

But not at that moment. It was one of the few clear days of the year. Mist had not come up and smoke did not escape from the chimneys since it was not yet dinnertime. In the course of their daily constitutional, the city appeared neatly etched out to the Syphon's members' eyes.

After the outing, Celso Viéitez, Merceditas' husband, the man who substituted imagination for method, would return home to continue his work of years on his wife's ancestry, the Valladares family. He was enlarging his sources every day. The *History of the Goths*, by Ourense's bishop, don Servando Souza, the church registry authenticated by cleric Gabriel de Pedro's *Peerage*, where he researched the Valladares' origins... He would unfailingly share his findings with Merceditas. He felt rewarded by her enthusiasm for her remote ancestors, all those knights of great consequence consorting with the nobility and even with Spanish and Portuguese Kings, taking part in wars, and in the Moorish conquest.

According to Celso's research, since medieval times the most enterprising branch of the Valladares family had ended up in Portugal. As he went further in his investigation, doubtful characters appeared in the family tree, having committed rape, incest, robbery and crime, like Xil Rodríguez, son of don Rodrigo Pais de Valladares and dona María Xil, died childless, murdered by Pedro Soares Gallinato. But this version contradicted another he had found in the *Portugal Description* by Duarte Nunhes. Here, Xil Rodríguez was shown as a "great magician" of supernatural powers who had signed a pact with the devil. He was indentured to the devil by a promissory note signed with his own blood. Having repented from his dealings with the devil, he lived a life of such intense penance that Our Lady herself had redeemed the Satanic document for him.

In Duarte Nunhes' book, Xil Rodriguez de Valladares had become friar Xil, venerated in Portugal for his exploits as a layman as for his miracles as a saint. He was buried in Santarem, in the convent of his order, and his day was celebrated May 14.

Merceditas much preferred this version this version to the one of the murdered Xil, of whom she wouldn't hear a word. She was ecstatic to find a saint in the family. When putting her son to bed every night, and after the 'Now I lay me down to sleep," she made him say a prayer to the family saint. She had invented the prayer herself: "Friar Xil, our ancestor, who was saved from Satan through the Virgin Mary, help me to keep myself pure and free from evil," or, "Saint Xil, as a proof of my love, I consecrate to you my eyes, my ears, my tongue, my heart, in a word, my whole being." The child repeated his mother's invocations every night, kneeling by his bed, hands together in angelic fervor. Convinced of the importance of blood ties, Merceditas trusted the protection of the saintly ancestor. She imagined him in heaven, dressed as a medieval knight but also wearing his holy crown, and looking down with pleasure upon these descendants who valued his intercession so highly. She had thought of making a pilgrimage to Santarem and, by exerting her family rights, to obtain a relic of Friar Xil. A scrap of his habit, a small page of his prayerbook, she saw it already enshrined in a portable chapel, like the one of Our Miraculous Lady that was brought to her every month, and to whom she lighted all these little candles on top of her dresser. She was so convinced of the protection of this family saint that in case of danger or fear, she would not exclaim O Lord Jesus! or O holy Lord! but O friar Xil! or May friar Xil succor us! Since she learned this version of the holiness of her ancestor she forbade her husband to continue his research for fear that the unmarried Xil, a shady character who got himself murdered by Pedro Soares perhaps after a brawl or a drunken revelry, would prevail over the other.

Celso knew that his wife disliked certain traits of her ancestors. Merceditas would have nothing to do with a Paio Soares de Valladares who had taken his wife by force, or don Lorenzo Soares de Valladares, already twice married and with plenty grown up daughters from both marriages, and who still had another daughter by his mistress, named also Sancha as his own wife. Merceditas could not bear this wantonness, particularly the bad taste of having a mistress with the same name as the legitimate wife. May Saint Xil spare me such humiliation! she thought. For when her husband would cry: Sancha my love, she would never know whether he was thinking of herself or of the other woman.

"Sancha was a common name then," Celso reassured her, "like Maruja now for example. Was it his fault, the coincidence?"

"What!!" snapped his wife, furious. "It was not his fault? You think it was all right for him to have a mistress, then?"

"No, no, love. I'm not saying that," contemporised the husband. "I meant it was a common name, that's all."

To calm her down, Celso talked of the nun daughters of that Lorenzo:

a dona Xana, prioress of the monastery and celibate, and two others, dona Constanza and dona Beatriz who were also nuns.

"They were legitimate, weren't they?" Merceditas wanted to know.

"Of course, from his second marriage," Celso hurried to explain avoiding the fact that another sister of those nuns, dona Aldonza, never married, but was Pero Fernandez de Castro's common law wife.

Merceditas had never wanted to hear anything else about this don Pedro, who happened to be a brother of the hypothetical saint, and ended his days at the hands of the law. This death was more befitting to the murdered Xil the sinner than to friar Xil the saint. Violent deaths seemed to be a family trait, due perhaps to the brothers aggressive or lewd conduct. Don Pedro was consequently erased from the Valladares family tree. On the other hand, abbess dona Luca, their half sister, was given due prominence as lofty companion to the Saint. Also the Saint's father, don Rodrigo Pais de Valladares, High Steward and Councillor of king don Sancho I of Portugal, later Lord Mayor of Coimbra. Since she heard of this figure, Merceditas would turn up the radio knob when she heard the *fado* 'Coimbra," the story of the fair Inés." The song told the story of the Galician Inés de Castro, crowned queen after her death. She quickly related her ancestor, the city mayor, to the ill–fated, beautiful Inés, since they were both Galegos. How much the good man would suffer with his fellow Galician's violent death! Merceditas would talk to her friends about the tragedy as if she had seen it. When her husband set to dissuade her, she was as unhappy as if someone in the family had died.

"Why can't it be as I say"?, she insisted. "They were both Galegos. They both lived there, in Coimbra. It is normal to think they met. And couldn't he help her, him a gentleman, and the city mayor besides? And her, a beautiful woman, so bewitching, who had the King round her little finger—The common land bonds"—went on Merceditas ponderously. "And he, being so powerful in Portugal, would not be unsympathetic. For he was a Galego, right? or so you said."

"There is no doubt on that score," said the husband in his role of accurate researcher, "the documents prove it."

"Well, then. Why couldn'it happen as I say?," insisted the wife.

"Because at the time of the Inés de Castro affair your ancestor, the mayor, had been long eaten up by worms," asserted Celso with authority.

Time was uncooperative. Merceditas had to renounce the romance concocted in her dreamy afternoons. It was a great pity, for the make believe family stories were her life's mainstay. Her husband was aware of this, and he doubled his efforts to trace glorious Valladares who would meet his wife's expectations.

In the half shadow of her sitting room, in the lethargy of the afternoon siesta, and surrounded by keepsakes, pictures, and her favorite ghosts, Merceditas summoned the past. From the radio of a near house came a song: 'Queen dona Costanza died, and all the people of Portugal, knowing she had died of grief, claimed for the death of Inés de Castro. She was condemned to death, and the sentence was carried out, leaving king don Pedro to live with a broken heart.' Since Celso, with admirable persistence and good will, had delved into all those documents to search for her ancestors, she felt all those historical characters closer to her. Who knows, maybe they were friends of the family. That king don Pedro, what a passion, Saint Xil!; dona Inés, what a beauty! She was so brave, even at the time of her execution, with her children crying round her skirts, trying to pull her back to life. And finally her severed head, so beautiful, with her hair loose like Veronica Lake...Oh, she sighed, letting her head roll on the headrest where it lied. The more familiar she became with her ancestors, the more understanding she grew toward their vices or excesses. When Celso, very prudently, told her a risqué tidbit on one of them, she still exclaimed: "How terrible! Please, Celso darling, do not tell me these things. It makes me sick here—pointing to her breast—and I cannot breathe." But deep inside it seemed that she was adjusting, their transgressions did not look so enormous any more. Human beings were like that, weak, she argued tolerantly, and the Valladares could do no less. Anything could happen. Even Saint Xil himself had been tempted by the Devil. Merceditas would reflect with certain smugness on the quirkiest motivations of all the Valladares sinners, trying to embellish them with psychological traits of her own making in such a way that, when talking to her friends of their misdeeds, it would seem that she had witnessed them personally.

Her friends would arrive later for the afternoon snack. That day they were coming with a guest, the wife of a Latin professor just arrived in

Lugo. The newcomer was from Pontevedra, but she looked out of the *Para Ti* magazine. Her hair in a big pompadour, she wore a Chartreux colored surach suit interspersed with black plaid. The biased skirt front was gathered on one side by a black satin ribbon forming a bow. She also wore a short jacket of the same material, with balloon sleeves and white piqué lapels. The jacket also had two black satin bows, matching the skirt.

Merceditas stole a quick glance at her, dwelling malevolently on her skirt, too short for provincial tastes, revealing her plump legs encased in nylon stockings, and her strap wedge shoes with black satin bows matching the skirt.

Fie, fie, Merceditas said to herself, breathing the stranger's lingering perfume when she approached for the customary rubbing of the cheeks. A fake, Merceditas thought, dressed fashionably but loudly. She could never dress like that. She thought slavish attachment to fashion bad taste. One has to know how to conform, her mother used to say. They, the Valladares, knew how to give fashion their personal touch, seeking balance, avoiding extravagance and trying always, of course, to look their best. Besides, one should strive for style. It was that touch of distinction that marked her family. She would look like a queen even in rags.

How smart you look, Merceditas! said her friends admiringly.

Please, don't say that. This is nothing but a simple frock, but very comfortable. It washes very well, and that is convenient for the country where one gets so dirty, she demurred coquettishly, looking like a doll.

She was wearing a navy blue light housedress, tucked at the waist, which made her figure slight and graceful. The white trimmed collar and cuffs softened the ensemble giving an impression of becoming neatness. Her well proportioned body was enhanced by her bare neck and her pulled back hair. She always wore her hair high but at night she would let it down, brushing her fair long curls with twenty strokes from their roots down in order to strengthen them. To Merceditas, who worshipped the real thing, the professor's wife was a conceited fake. A fashion plate, no doubt, but so vulgar. One only had to look at her. She was wearing a ton of makeup...Friar Xil! She had been afraid to stick when they perfunctorily kissed. That woman stank of Ponds cream.

They had hot chocolate with biscuits in gold ribbed porcelain cups.

The newcomer made a face at the slightly rancid biscuits. That house, she thought, and those people were a little passé. The smell of insecticide increased her sensation of distaste.

"With this heat the flies are so persistent," commented their host, "not even the Flit can do away with them."

The visitor felt a certain admiration for high born people, but they all smelled of parchment to her. She had been introduced to the group by Julianita, the wife of one of her husband's colleagues, and they in turn invited her to meet with Merceditas.

The conversation was in full swing, the other women encouraging her to go on. She said she had a wedding in Pontevedra next month, the daughter of a magistrate. She had been with her at Placeres school, and now was marrying a Navy ensign. The reception would be in Marin, at the Naval Academy, and would include a gala ball.

"They look so smart in uniform, don't they?" said Marujita, a fright, according to Merceditas, but as nice and obliging there was none like her. "Those white gloves, always so immaculate, and their hanging swords..."

"Smashing!," agreed the visitor wholeheartedly. "The girls are crazy about them. Besides, they are so distinguished, so attentive..."

"And how come you didn't nab one for yourself, honey?," said Manolita, a real scream.

"Well, let me tell you. I didn't lack beaux...I remember that on my debutante ball I danced with more than one, and I was asked out many times...But"—she abandoned the dreamy tone—"our fate is always sealed. Xenaro, my husband, was a friend of the family. Like my father said: he is a man of consequence, serious, dependable, and will treat you like a queen...And here I am—"she said matter-of-factly—. "Of course, I lack nothing."

"Come on, come on...And he is a lot older than you, isn't he?" hinted Manolita.

"Yes, fifteen years," answered the guest.

More likely not even ten, but she wants to pass herself off as a girl, thought Merceditas.

"What will you wear at the wedding?," insisted Marujita.

"A green organza dress that I have ordered."

"Woman dressed in green, her beauty on a dare." quoted Manolita half mockingly half in earnest.

"Trimmed with Valenciennes lace"—went on the other ignoring the quip—"and a ruchée collecting the skirt flounce. I will accessory with a tulle shawl in the same shade. They are so becoming, right? and one feels so good embraced by them..."

"By whom? asked Merceditas malevolently.

"The shawls, of course,"—answered the woman embarrassed.

"Organza, musseline, chiffon, all those gossamer fabrics are good for younger women. As for us, we look better in thicker materials: taffeta, faye, satin, or silk crêpe which folds down so nicely...They are more lady-like—" says Merceditas underlining the lady part.

"What to it? Youth is a mental state," said Marujita evenly.

"Perhaps, but our bodies say differently," contradicted her host ironically.

"What are you sewing?," asked Marujita picking up some pants from the sewing basket and thus trying to change the conversation.

"Don't ask," rued Merceditas. "The milkwoman put me on the spot. She wants me to shorten her husband's trousers...I am so sorry for the poor woman, she is having such a hard time..."

"I can help you if you wish, dear. I am rather good at it," offered Marjua.

"Isn't it true that she has Merle Oberon's eyes?" asked Manolita à propos of nothing while pointing at the visitor.

This Manolita always so dense. She has fish eyes, rather, thought Merceditas to whom the newcomer was not pleasing.

"Have you seen *Eternal Ties* by Deanna Durbin?" asked the woman, perhaps by way of new comparison since the Merle Oberson reference did not seem to make her too happy.

"No, it hasn't been out yet. Honey, here movies take ages to release! But the other day, at the 'España,' we saw *It happened in China* by Myrna Loy and Clark Gable," said Maruja.

"Oh, Clark Gable!," exclaimed the newcomer. "What a man!"

"I never get to see his movies. My husband doesn't like them," complained Manolita.

"Sweetie, why don't you go by yourself? If it were the opposite, nothing would stop him from going," said the woman showing off her modern leanings.

"I wish I could, believe me, but I don't dare. You don't know this town. You'll see. They criticize you for every little thing. So one has to be very careful," stated Manolita resignedly, opening slightly her Cupid-bow lips and dabbing at the lipstick on them with a slender finger.

"You care too much about others. Women are becoming liberated all over the world," said the visitor taking the silver compact out of her handbag and patting her nose with the puff.

"Martin, my husband," explained Marujita, "told me that he has read in 'O Progreso' that in England a woman was appointed minister of Food, a doctor Edith something..."

"In England, for sure," said Merceditas pointedly. "Here we don't go beyond the busybodies of the Sección Femenina."

Wisely Maruja changed the topic. She didn't know yet the newcomer's political affiliation.

"What are you reading?," she asked picking up a book from a coffee table.

"*It is not Love*, by Barcia," answered Merceditas. "Celso gave it to me the other day."

"Who is he?," asked the visitor holding it in her hands.

"A writer from here, from Lugo. One should keep up with the neighbors."

"By the way," cut in Maruja. "I just started *Loving Heights*..."

"You mean *Wuthering Heights*?" said the woman.

"No. Here we are more original, we change storms into love."

"See," said Merceditas without restraining her antagonism. "It is also a novel by a local writer, Antonio Quintela Ferreiro."

"Who knows what that nut can scribble!," cried Manolita. "He is a crazy loon. He lives in fear of being poisoned, and mistrusts everybody, even his own mother."

"That's right. Celso told me that he always wears gloves, even indoors, to avoid touching anything poisonous."

A blond child in a sailor suit and patent leather shoes barges in like lightning and flings himself into Merceditas arms.

"Ummmmm!," Merceditas hugged him. "How this little boy loves his Mama!" She rains little kisses on his cheeks. "Let's see—," she looks at him. "How dirty you look! Off to the bathroom with you, my lamb. María!" she called. "Draw the bath for Baby! How could you let him carry on so! You should have watched him carefully"—she said reproachfully to the nanny when she appeared at the drawing room door in her black uniform and white apron.

"Yes Ma'am, right now. Little boys are like monkeys, they do not mind us," replied the nanny apologetically.

"That means they are healthy and strong," says the guest with authority. "Come here. What is your name?", she inquires fussing over him.

"Juanjo," piped the child in the sweetest voice.

"Did you have a good time? Did you play a lot?" she asks.

"I had to play dummy once at tag, y'know" explains the child.

"Careful, Juan José, or you will make that lady all dirty," cautions Merceditas pulling him away from the woman, thinking that it was rather her son who would be contaminated by her. "Go for your bath, sweetheart. You look like a ragamuffin."

The flustered child leaves running, holding in his hand the coin that her mother's friend just gave him.

"Look what I got, tata," he shows his nanny while she starts undressing him in the bathroom. "I will buy me licorice."

He thought that woman quite nice, not only for the coin but because she didn't slobber over him like all the others.

Back in the drawing room, the women were ecstatic over the child.

"What a beautiful child!" says the visitor with sincerity. "His eyes! His curls! If he were a girl he would be another Shirley Temple."

"He is a little charmer," says Manolita while wiping lipstick traces from the corners of her Cupid bow mouth. "And his mother dresses him so nicely."

"Sure thing," says another. "He always looks like out of the bandbox."

"Bah, bah, you exaggerate," says Merceditas drooling.

"And he looks so delicate, so well mannered"— says the newcomer.

"He is a know-it-all, that's for sure," agrees the mother. "And always so loving. He is a blessing to his father and I."

"It's great when they turn out like this, dear. A good son is priceless," says Manolita sententiously.

As a summoned spirit, the child's father appeared across the hall with his solemn air. As usual, he greets them from the door, to avoid cutting into the conversation. He makes for his study where he spends normally a couple of hours among his wife's family
papers but Merceditas stops him.

"Celso, look, I want to introduce to you Mrs..." She hesitates.

"Hermida," points out the new guest with a shaky voice. She is clearly impressed by the man's looks, and by the way he bows his head while kissing her hand.

"She is the wife of the new professor of Latin," explains Merceditas.

After a few pleasantries, the man excuses himself soberly and leaves the room.

Silence ensued after his leaving. All of them are smitten by him, guessed Merceditas wryly. They were eating him up with their eyes. Usually, when the time comes for him to return home, she notices the anxiety of her friend's glances, the restlessness of their limbs. They think I am not aware of it. Those harpies! That awful woman even blushed when he held her hand to say hello. Well, let them suffer. Nothing doing.

In the bathroom, the nanny dries the child with a big towel and sprays La Toja talcum powder over his little bottom.

"You have another blue," she points to his leg. "You are all mauled up, black and blue. And it's because you are very naughty," scolds María.

"Look tata, I'm a little nun...," says the child in front of the mirror wrapping himself in the towel. "And now," he covered his mouth with the towel leaving only his eyes out, "I am the girl from the "Thief of Baghdad.""

"Who?" asked María.

"You don't know who the "Thief of Baghdad" was?"

"I don't care. Thieves are no good people," she scoffs, her left eye crossing a little.

"This one was. He had a magic flying carpet. The girl was a princess and she lived in a palace like this," he picks a box of "Oriental

Woods" compact powder from a shelf. "You see the picture? They live here, and they wear turbans..."

"Bosh!... Wait here, I forgot your pajamas," says María leaving the room running.

Juanjo takes advantage of the nanny's absence to get ahold of his mother's lipstick and smudge it on his lips.

"What are you doing? I cannot leave you out of my sight for a minute. This is woman's stuff. If your Papa sees you doing this —" scolds María while rubbing vigorously the red off his lips.

The child continues to watch himself in the mirror.

"I want to be like Mama, as beautiful as Mama..."

"But you are already! You are your mother's likeness for sure . I never saw anything like it...Sweet Jesus!," and she kisses him loudly.

"Ouch!" whines the child hurt by the rough kiss.

"Saint Mollycoddle, having babies through her fingers," teases María.

In the kitchen she warms up his soup and puts it on the table. She takes a bottle from the shelf and fills up a spoon with a thick fluid. She takes it to him, and the child backs away. It is cod liver oil.

"I don't want to!," cries the child.

"Come on. This one is for Mama..." says María, coming closer.

"I don't like it! Buah!" the child is adamant.

"If you take it, you'll become a big man, like Papa," cajoles María.

"Shan't!"

"Shall I call your Mama?" threatens the nanny.

"No! Don't call her," cries the child.

"Well, then—" she takes the spoon to his mouth.

"Sing to me 'The little paper house,'" begs the little lad.

"We'll spend all our nights by the moonlight, while living in our little paper house...," sings María while pressing his nostrils with two fingers.

"That's more like it," says María giving him a piece of lemon to wash away the bad taste from his mouth.

Chapter 2

Juanjo went through every childhood disease. When he had the whooping cough he had to be taken to Monterroso, to some friends' house, since Lugo's winter fog, hanging for days over the city, would have choked him to death. He won't get over it, thought Merceditas, this cough will tear him apart. When he had the measles, they hung a red light in his room to protect his feverish eyes. German measles, said his mother, had left a mark which fortunately, would not be visible when his eyebrow grew to adult size. When they took his First Communion picture, in a real sweet Admiral costume, she hid it under face powder. Hot linseed poultices were applied to his chest to soften his recurrent bronchitis. Although he never went out in the street without his woollen cap, he suffered frequent earaches. How patient he was, my dear angel baby, to suffer the hot pads his mother applied to his ears. Merceditas soaked a soft cloth, a piece of very old fabric, into a small pan of boiling water placed on his bedside table. She would blow softly on her burned fingers to alleviate the heat, and, after wringing the cloth, she held it by the corners pressing it against the aching ear. Hold on a little, my king, she said, you'll see how the pain goes away. And it was true, more so for her love than for the hot pads. Another time he came to suffer continuous tummy trouble that would not stop with grated apples or anything else. The pediatrician could not understand the cause of that persistent diarrhea till it was discovered that the kid was pigging out on his father's Laxen Busto pills swiped from their small red tin box. The pills looked like silver foil wrapped chocolates, and naughty Juanjo would feast on them on the sly. They took away the box of Laxen Busto, and the diarrhea stopped.

He went through all the illnesses, but he got over them, growing always a few inches taller after each time.

Twice his costume had won first prize in the children's Carnival. Once, dressed as a Moor, with wide silk pantaloons, Turkish slippers, a golden sequinned embroidered vest, and a white turban with grandfather's ruby tie clasp, just for the picture. For the ball he wore a fake shiny diamond brooch which produced even a better effect. Merceditas had applied dark makeup to disguise his naturally white skin, so unMoorish like. He wore lipstick and his eyes were lined with black mascara. Even so, two bright blue eyes shone strangely in the fake blackness of Juanjo's face. What a handsome Moor! cried his mother, contemplating her masterpiece. His mother wanted to dress him up as a prince, but he had insisted that he wanted to be a Moor. Those days he was obsessed by the Moors. He would sit easily on the floor in Moorish fashion, legs crossed, after practicing for a week. He also learned how to salute touching his face slightly with his right hand, just like the movies. He pestered the fourth floor tenant, a veteran of the Ifni sharp shooters regiment during the Moorish wars, to teach him the Arabic greeting. The gentlemen could hardly explain to Juanjo that the poor cannon fodder Arabs he met at the Segre front had nothing to do with the Moor Juanjo had in mind. 'Jamalajama' he said to keep him quiet, and the kid repeated it with a flourish of his arm when called onstage to pick up his prize.

"How cute!" a lady said to Merceditas. "If Cesáreo González sees him, surely he'll make him a movie star, honey. What a panache! He is scared of nothing. Mine on the contrary—" she rued looking at a serious looking young kid sitting by her side—"is a bear."

Juanjo exchanged short pants for plus fours. He stopped playing cops and robbers with the gang at the park and ogled the girls strolling together by the Rúa da Reina. In secret, he still read Roberto Alcázar and his sidekick Pedrín's comics even though they were kid stuff. He went from seeking Pedrín's likeness—how many hours in front of the mirror to achieve his forelock!—to Roberto Alcázar's, so sure of himself, so attractive...But Juanjo had nothing to be jealous for. He looked like a hunk. Absolutely tops. Blond, with wavy hair, blue eyed, a well-delineated mouth, straight nose, rather short for a man's, perfect teeth, a sweet smile, perhaps a little naïve despite his manly mien. He was his mother's perfect likeness, but he had his father's figure. He was a true male model. Merceditas thought Lugo's stores too provincial, and she traveled regularly to A Coruña to buy him clothes. She favored

Andrés Feal, the best Corunese tailor, who had Franco himself among his customers.

María, his nanny, no longer watched his bath or his crossdressings, but these went on nevertheless. Juanjo profited from his parents' absences to go into their room, open his mother's closet and pick up an outfit to strut about in. Those moments were for him more attractive than walking with friends, talking to girls, parties, everything. He preferred above all Merceditas creamy satin ball dress, trimmed around the neckline with small glass beads, and a valance at the hem of the skirt. When he put the dress on, he would inhale delightedly its odor, a mixture of sweat, 'Oriental Woods' and the mothballs in which it was stored. The pungent, almost unpleasant smell became the headiest of aromas for him. His feet would not fit into the low heeled shoes though. He opened the music jewel box and fingered his mother's rings, the engagement diamond bracelet that went so well with the dress, and he danced to the ever slowing music of *The Blue Danube* coming from the box. As he danced around, he raised his arms, encased in long satin gloves, to hold other uncertain hands with which he danced a minuet. When the music wound up, he curtsied Versailles–like; and with a shy smile, he bowed his saucy curls at the hypothetical male dance partner. Afterwards, he donned a fox cape, and he caressed the fur letting it slid between his fingers. Sitting on a pouff in front of the dresser's oval mirror he made up his face, putting lipstick on and blackening his eyebrows slightly with a pencil, rubbing his finger under his lower eyelashes the way his mother did. Studying his face, he looked at his reflection in the mirror smiling with pleasure. Getting up slowly, he would come close to the mirror and kiss his own mouth, pressing hard against the glass. He liked to feel its coldness warm up to the touch of his lips. He looked at the traces of his mouth and cried admiratively: 'How much I like you!' He would sing rapturously: 'How pretty you are, how precious...' with his unsteady, unbroken adolescent voice. Juanjo knew he was handsome, the prettiest one after Mama. You'll never touch or kiss anyone more beautiful, he said to himself while letting his hands caress the soft fabric, hugging his body with pleasure. He kissed his naked shoulders and arms, feeling himself harden with desire. He would masturbate looking at his own reflection, making faces like a lascivious maiden—no one like me, ever!—. While the image on the mirror became blurred, his eyes veiled—now touch yourself like this, oh yes!—and he would slump on the carpet, holding on to the pouff, twisting with pleasure.

He would clean up thoroughly afterwards to avoid any traces. Just thinking of his mother finding out about all that made his heart freeze in terror. No one would ever know. His confessor, Father Puga, wanted to know. Do you engage in impure touching? At night? In bed? How? Tell me, son—and Juanjo felt the old man's hot breath and the sweatdrops falling from his forehead—how do you do it, son? he urged, letting his fingers slide over the top of his head. Put your trust in God, son, and then he would hold Juanjo's hands between his sweaty palms, ugh, how gross. If at least he would not sweat so...

He changed priests, to no avail. They were all the same. They wanted to know. He remained close mouthed. When pressed, he made up lies. Besides he did not repent. He said his penance, three Our Father, three Hail Marys and three Glory to the Father, or Blessed Be Your Purity, to fight those transgressions imagined by the priest, but never confessed by Juanjo. He knew he would fall again into the same vice, into his solitary delight.

He finished high school at Fingoi, but further schooling was not attractive to him. He wanted to be a poet like his ancestors, the Galician-Portuguese troubadours whose poems his mother had shown to him. Look, son, the great medieval poets belonged to our family! Merceditas had been compensated of the Inés de Castro fiasco when Celso, her husband, found out that Sueiro Airas Valladares was a son of Airas Nunes who had also fathered Joan Airas. Two of the greatest troubadours of the Galician-Portuguese poetry of the thirteenth century were among his ancestors. See, son, Airas Nunes himself, the greatest poetic genius of his time, a collaborator of king Alfonso X the Wise's book, the "Cantigas to Our Lady."

When this was discovered by Celso, the Syphon tertulia had a lot to say about it. The fact that his wife was a distant relative of such famous medieval poets gave Celso greater stature amoung his peers, even with those who thought him too stuffy and serious minded. They saw Celso's company more appropriate for the senate tertulia and its bigshots like

Pérez Guerra, Vázquez Seijas, Narciso Peinado and such, who were the cream of Lugo is high society. But the subject of medieval poetry put Celso on the spotlight, removing the label of dullness from him. Opinions varied, though, for in the tertulia there were several experts in the field.

"Even Teófilo Barga confuses Joan Arias with Airas Nunes. Same thing with dona Carolina Michaëlis de Vasconcelos..."

"I have read that they were contemporaries rather than father and son."

There was a big snag to consider Joan Airas to be Airas Nunes son: the latter was a priest. Someone suggested to consult Carré Aldao's book; others to write Xosé María Alvarez Blázquez in Vigo to throw some light into the matter. The subject was impressive and gave much to talk about.

"I mean, what if he was a priest? I mean, he wouldn't be the first priest to have children, right?" said don Cesáreo, his big paunch quivering with laughter.

"Priests who do not have sons have nephews," said don Lino sarcastically.

"Of course. They have housekeepers not wives," said Figueroa.

"But, I mean, they are not made of stone. I mean, they also have their heart of hearts..."

"That Airas Nunes most of all. You only have to read his love poems," said don Lino.

"I don't know about that. Love poems in the Middle Ages were rather conventional. They obeyed fixed rules..."—pointed out Celso Viéitez.

"Just formally," insisted don Lino, "but through their content we can infer the poets' lives and feelings and even the customs and history of the times. I remember Fermín Bouza Brey when writing *The Lonely Ship* had commented how close he felt to those men, despite the time difference."

"One has to remember that the Church was an outlet for the nobility, especially second sons. Religious vocation came in second place," opined the historian.

"The Church was the depositary of cultural life," said Trapero.

"Should our bishop, don Rafael Balauzá and Navarro be here, he would engage in one of his politico–cultural tirades favoring the Church over the barbaric and ignorant state power..." said Figueroa.

"By the way," cut in Ibáñez who had just got back from Madrid. "Is it true that he did not allow the Caudillo enter the Cathedral under the canopy?"

"Sure. This bishop is a rebel. If all were like him, even I would go to Mass..."

"They shot his brother, and he can't forgive that. That's what it is."

"Our bishops are rather a breed apart," argued Ibáñez.

"Sure they are. From that first one, Odoario, we had them in every shape: Aryans, Priscilians, insurgents...Our history is our bishops'," said don Lino. "They had power, and ruled the town for centuries..."

"I mean, they still do, God help us. Lugo is still a bishop's fief."

"But, coming back to the medieval poet..."

"Arias Nunes," helped Celso.

"It is clear that being a priest was not a hindrance to write love poems, or to carry carnal love to the logical outcome," said Figueroa.

"It could be even a Galician tradition. Our saintly Rosalía de Castro's father, as you know, was a priest, a don..."

"Let's not confuse the issue," said don Cesáreo inflicting a new brandy stain on his shirt. "I can see your intention to declare that priests are born poets, and I mean, although our village priest has a passel of sons around the parish, I cannot see a single poet among them..."

Celso Viéitez tried to hide his discomfort with the general laughter on a matter so important to him. Don Lino could not repress his guffaws, although he knew how to keep the conversation on a higher plane.

"Of course, Arias Nunes and Joan Airas have in common being fine poets; also our irony, the Galician retranca. But without malice or slander, unlike many other poets of their time."

"I still doubt they were father and son. Airas Nunes' high morals are prominent in his poems. He shows clearly his indignation when his niece, a dona Sancha Rodríguez de Segamondi, was abducted by a relative, a Gallinato," said Trapero.

"Abduction was not unusual at that time," showed off Celso. "Even among the nobility. I have found several cases in my wife's ancestry, but you will understand that I had to overlook the subject...," he shrugged sheepishly, seeking male understanding towards his wife's scruples.

"But Airas Nunes," insisted Trapero, "always denounces violent conduct."

"I mean," said Cesáreo spraying cigar ashes all over his stained shirtfront— "no one said here that he begot his son in violence, damn it! It might very well be that the other part consented freely. If he was so good with his pen, I mean, well, he could be just as good with his rod, I mean..."

"This is not here nor there," said Trapero rising his voice over the general hilarity. Even the enthused card players back at the corner turned their eyes towards them. "I tell you even more," he elaborated when everyone grew calmer. "Arias Nunes even wrote a moral satire, something quite unusual in our poetry, the one that begins: "Since truth has grown smaller in the world..."

The subject of medieval poetry lasted several days. Celso Viéitez complicated things more and more as he went along with his research. He found out that Paio Soares, Joan Airas nephew, and therefore a grandson of Airas Nunez, was also an important poet. It seemed that poetry was a family trait.

Merceditas could not restrain her delight. Nothing could please her more than to have artistic ancestors. And so glorious as those! Her husband had hidden the ecclesiastical calling of the father from her to avoid trouble. But now with the newest finds, fresh 'moral' problems would arise. It seemed to Celso that those Valladares would stop at nothing.

That new Paio Soares was not as prolific as his ancestors nor were his poems so perfect, and he supplied the Syphon with much thought. In her *Randglossen*, dona Carolina Michaëlis de Vasconcelos proved that Paio Soares was the author of a love poem, precisely the one numbered thirty eight in the *Ajuda Love Songbook*, in which he mentions his beloved. That fortunate lady was no less the famous María Pais de Ribeiro, the celebrated 'Ribeiriña.'

"That Ribeiriña, wasn't she the mistress of King Sancho I of Portugal?. 'How I long for my friend in A Guarda,' quoted don Lino.

"The same, answered Celso with an enthusiasm unusual in him." And not only the king's. She turned the heads of many knights of the time."

"Look at her, the little slut!" said Figueroa.

"But what is the big deal? If she was so famous, it is normal that Soares would dedicate a poem to her..."

"Not so normal, not so normal," argued don Lino maliciously. "Celso's research has put the matter in quite a different light," he added with a dry laugh.

They all looked at Celso who fumbled with his tie knot before speaking diffidently.

"Contrary to the opinion of Cesare de Llolis, dona Carolina had already surmised that Ribeiriña was a relative of the elder Soares. According to my own research," and he couldn't help sounding a bit pompous, "that María Pais de Valladares had entered a second marriage with Martín Pais de Ribeira. The nickname could be due to her husband. There is no proof of issue from this marriage."

"Dona Carolina affirms that she had a son by king don Sancho I, who would also become a troubadour," said Trapero.

"What an accomplished family, I mean..."

"Let Celso finish," commanded don Lino.

"Brief, the complication lies in Pais being, either Ribeiriña's father by his marriage to dona Elvira Vasques de Severosa, or her nephew, the son of María's brother, don Sueiro Pais."

"That is to say that either way we are confronted with an incestuous relationship," said Figueroa rubbing his hands.

"The fact that he dedicated poems to her doesn't prove anything. I mean, poets do let their imagination run wild," said Cesáreo drawing avidly from his cigar.

"Let's say that it was an incestuous poem, then," agrees Figueroa.

A few days later, and after having checked some sources, don Lino produced Cesare de Llolis' quote in *A tribute to M. Pidal*: "The kinship between the troubadour and the beautiful lady has never been proven..."

"You see? Llolis cannot conceive that a medieval poet can sing the praises of a lady relative."

"According to my own research, there is no doubt they did." argued Celso seriously.

"Maybe there was another María Pais..."

"Ribeiriña," went on don Lino, "had an adventurous life. The critic says that after king don Sancho I's death, she became passionately in love with a Lourenco de Alvarenga."

"She awakened uncontrollable passions..."

"What a pity abduction has become obsolete now. I know of some women that..."

"Abduction is out, I mean, after the Sabine women, people do not..."

"There are some who still practice it as a rule. Think of the gypsies," interjected don Lino.

"Continuing with Ribeiriña's story," insisted Celso, not renouncing his researcher's rights, "the matter does not end there. Later on she married don Joan Fernandez de Lima and had four children by him."

"What a dame! She still had strength left. Those were real women, by Jove!"

"I am not surprised with Soares, despite being her nephew..."

"Yeah, better her nephew than her father..."

"I don't understand those prejudices. Whom should one love more than his own daughter? Besides, it's all in the family."

"Of course. Everything clicks together. Here in our country we have more incestuous relationships than we think. In the villages...children and grandchildren...like this!" said don Lino making a pineapple with his right hand.

"And let's not forget the custom of marrying cousins."

"Cousins, close ones," points out Figueroa.

As it was not unusual, the conversation degenerated into nonsense. At that moment it was hard to keep it on track. But the incest topic was too stimulating to let go, and it came up again in subsequent tertulias.

"It has been scientifically proven that incestuous relationships produce abnormal offspring. Incest is not a moral taboo, it's sound prophylactic practice," stated Trapero.

"I don't think so." Don Lino enjoyed being antagonistic if he had sufficient arguments. "Incest was severely punished even with death in primitive societies. And not only they had no concept of moral law, but they were not aware of modern scientific facts. Proof of this is that the greatest leniency was father–daughter incest."

"I mean, in Egypt, even the Pharaohs married their own sisters, didn't they?"

"The incest taboo is mostly social. The prohibition was established to facilitate exogamy, to enlarge the group and procure more working hands, or to make allies out of possible enemies. I believe that is the main reason."

All the theories were of no help to Celso. His only concern was how to inform his wife about this new development of her ancestors.

He would not be so worried had he known Merceditas overlooked the more risqué aspects to concentrate only in what interested her. The most important medieval poets were Valladares. That was the only thing that counted for her.

She would show the poems to her son, instilling in him the desire of being a poet. But Juanjo wanted more to be an actor. To play different roles, to dress up in wigs or whatever, to go onstage and receive afterwards the applause of an adoring public, bravo! his dressing room overfilling with flowers. An actor could apply makeup openly in front of a big mirror from a dresser chock full of cosmetics, rather than hiding in his mother's bedroom as he used to do when home alone.

His father's hopes to send him to the university were soon dashed. He had reservations about any career. Law? So vulgar and monotonous...Pharmacy? No way; the students were all village girls anyway...Medicine? But Papa, I just faint at the sight of blood! I couldn't bear all those TB patients coughing in my face...Besides, I would be sick all the time. You know I catch everything under the sun."

"It looks like Juan José is never going to do anything serious with his life," said Celso worriedly to his wife. "He should have a proper education..."

"Yes, dear," acquiesced Merceditas lightly. "Yes, but..." she supported her son, "he has some reasons. College is so uninspiring! He has such imagination, and he is so sensitive too...!"

"You could make him go, if you wanted to," said Celso cutting short his wife's surmise. "But the truth is that you don't. You refuse to give him up. And it would be beneficial for him, you know. He is a Mama's boy, always hanging onto your skirts..."

"You are not jealous, are you?" cooed Merceditas hugging him. She was trying to pacify him, showing herself sweet and loving. "Don't be silly. I am proud of our relationship. He is not like other sons who want nothing to do with their parents or their home. Better having him close by, you know. There are so many sneaky girls trying to catch him...And he is still so young, so naïve...an angel,!" she finished closing her eyes as if smelling a strong perfume....

"I am not silly, He knows how to have you round his little finger, that's for sure...But he doesn't show any inclination to be a real man," said Celso with a dreary air.

Her husband was right. Merceditas did not encourage her son to go to college. She couldn't bear the thought of parting from him. Just to think about it her heart grew so heavy that she suffocated. Saint Xil forbid! Nothing could compare to her relationship with her son. Celso, her husband, was so serious, so uninteresting...He was a good man, a good provider, and always attentive...but apart from his work on the family tree, he didn't have any other graces. Lately his research had advanced, and thanks to the scholar Blas de Nasarre he had learned that the Valladares' blood went back to Fonta Walcario and his wife Gliscamunda, a daughter to emperor Theodosius. Merceditas was somewhat disconcerted with this Gothic, barbarian new blood running through her veins. Of course, Mama, that's why we have Nordic, blue eyes, said Juanjo. Merceditas was not too sanguine, but the fact that the Valladares family held kings, even emperors, could not be gainsaid.

The Valladares saga. Juanjo was so familiar with it that he knew all the traits and idiosyncrasies of the grandparents and great-grandparents he had never known. Through his mother stories, he walked the pazo's corridors; he drank Uncle Ramón's liqueurs; he saw his reflection among the water lilies and lotuses of the pond while he listened to the atonal concert of the gliding doves. He read the medieval poems under the shade of the birchtrees flanking the driveway; he perceived the thrushes filling up the valley like a mist. He felt Saladina's kisses and saw the pockmarks on her cheeks. His mother's experiences became his own.

Besides real people, all those ancestors discovered thanks to his father's research, became domestic, friendly ghosts for him. Queens, noblemen, court ladies, sworded knights...all the trappings of courtly life would parade in a mental minuet during mother and son conversations.

They even acted out many episodes of their lives, like the death challenge between a Valladares and another nobleman—a villain—a rival for the affection of his beloved. Like Errol Flynn, Juanjo used his mother's knitting needles to fight his rival to death. The game became furiously paced. You scoundrel!, he sneered while plunging his sword into his enemy's heart. His beloved, Merceditas, watched the flight with trembling heart from a recess of the castle walls half covered with a mantilla. With her face partly hidden by a rag from her sewing basket, she collapsed into a chair, then slided down to the floor to make the fainting more real. Discarding his sword with a flourish Juanjo switched from avenging knight to caring lover. He picked up his mother from the floor avoiding to look at her thighs, exposed when her skirt got caught in the chair. He tried not to bump into her tits when he helped her up, not to bring her body too close to his own so that he wouldn't burn with her warmth nor feel her breath so near his mouth...But even so, he would feel the upheaval of his heart beating furiously. He would lead his mother to the sofa, pretending to be worn out by the performance. Merceditas' red face and gaspings for air, resembling more a fainting spell, were too intense for a simple theatrical performance. Their nervous laughter masked their uneasiness, and the scene was over.

Friar Xil's ecstasies in his Santarem cell were also reenacted. Merceditas would improvise a makeshift tunic and Juanjo, kneeling, adopted a mystical countenance while his mother recited from the Kempis prayerbook.

More than a saint, Juanjo preferred to play the valiant Cid riding into Moorish lands. He also thought of the Masked Warrior, with his big cross over his heart, conquering kingdoms for Christianity. Merceditas could play the wife, saying her farewells from the castle's battlements, her eyes full of tears—o, my love is leaving me, how sad—or a Moorish captive that the warrior freed and protected, more for being a woman than an enemy. The Valladares magnanimity remained always unsullied.

One of their best dramatizations was that of the poem of the shepherdess of Crecente Grove by Joan Airas. Merceditas made up long tresses, plaiting her own hair with yellow wool, and completing her costume with a peasant's headdress. Carrying her sewing basket on the crook of her arm she would pretend picking daisies on her country walk, 'at sunup by the banks of the Sar.' She sang a weak soprano while picking the imaginary flowers: 'In the green lane, that green lane leading to the hermitage, daisies cry of grief because you left.' She squatted to pick up the flowers, and all of a sudden Juanjo the knight, appeared. He removed his plumed hat and bowed his head almost to the ground where the beautiful shepherdess had been surprised singing in solitude:

> My lady, to you I must
> Speak
> A little, by your leave.
> But if you will me so,
> This place I will depart.

Upon seeing the knight Merceditas would blush shyly, suppressing a startled cry, her hand over her mouth. Hesitantly, afraid of what others might think, she replied:

> O, Sire, by Our Lady,
> Do not remain here any longer,
> But go on quickly on your way.
> You will do the right thing
> To anybody in these parts.
> Since if you are found here
> They will say it is my fault.

'My lady,' obeyed Juanjo leaving the scene after bidding the woman farewell with utmost respect. She was left behind desolate to see him go, stretching out her arm, anxious to detain him, her silent cry to stop him never uttered.

This skit had been even performed in front of Merceditas' lady friends, who had applauded warmly, finding it extremely edifying.

This was the start of Juanjo's career as an actor.

Besides the Valladares' lore, mother and son shared confidences on Juanjo's outings, walks, parties and even his love conquests. Merceditas was his advisor, polishing his tastes up to the well known sophistication of the Valladares family. Any young lady crossing Juanjo's path she found fault with. One was a little coarse, the other too wild; another had bandy legs; another was too conceited and, after all, who was she, a nobody...It seemed that in the whole area it could not be found a woman worthy of her angel. Who could match his grace and sympathy, thought his mother with conviction. Through her son she could live things she had been unable to do as a woman: sampling around till finding her ideal of a man. Through his mother, Juanjo fed on flattery, that ego's nourishment which turned him into the most feared Don Juan of the region.

He never had time to carry out his mothers well-heeled designs. Fate intervened altering his course. A gorgeous creature came to cut short Juanjo's Don Juan's career. That beautiful child, with her narrow waist enhanced by the starched can-can petticoats she wore, was a princess, a new Sissi. She had taken Lugo by storm. She was visiting her aunt, a Pimentel. She had been brought up in France, by Catholic nuns, of course, and she was as well mannered as a true señorita should. She had fallen from heaven like a meteor creating havoc in the peaceful Lucense community. All admiring eyes were fastened on the girl. In coffee shops, at homes, in the market place, the young lady's life and miracles were widely discussed. It was said that she spoke French and English; she played the piano; she had a lovely voice, and it was heavenly to listen to her singing Schubert's 'Ave María.' She had given her aunt a tablecloth and matching napkins embroidered by herself. Her wardrobe was a dream, all French, of course. She was a modern girl but also traditional in many ways. Her aunt had said that she had many suitors: diplomats, engineers, the best matches...Nobody talked of anything else. Young men looked at her as at Our Lady of the Pillar, up on a pedestal, away from their reach.

For Juanjo it meant a challenge. He employed all his wiles: the piercing gaze that drove women crazy; his elegance and sex appeal, the pressure of his arm when holding her waist; the whispering in her ear while dancing; "I am anxious to hold you in my arms..." Araceli, that was the Frenchie's name, fell madly in love with him.

Nor her looks nor her family could be at fault this time. She looked like a princess. She was a niece of the Pimentel's. She had enough family crests as not to beg the Valladares for anything. According to Celso, who rushed to delve into her family tree—it was beginning to be a dangerous obsession for him—the Pimentels were noblemen going back to king Alfonso VI. One of them had gone to Portugal accompanying the king's rebellious grandson, the one who would later become king Alfonso Enriques, the conqueror of Lisbon. Another Martín Pimentel had participated in the conquest of Seville. They had married into royal families. On that account Merceditas had nothing to say but still she was hoping to find some trick to free her son from such an entanglement.

"They look like a couple out of a movie," commented Merceditas' friends.

"Don't they though?" she agreed with false gaiety.

"It looks like it's serious, what?" they hinted with malice.

"My, my, what a bunch of matchmakers...This is puppy love. They are still so young! Who knows what life may bring!" she reassured herself.

"Your son could have done worse. Aunt Pimentel must have a big wad..."

"All ways lead to money," kidded Manolita trying to be clever.

That kidding around drove Merceditas crazy. She hoped all that stuff would not last beyond the summer. But the children advanced from bolero songs and tender gazes to more dangerous games. The Frenchie got herself knocked up. Aunt Pimentel ran to speak to Merceditas who almost fainted at the news.

"This girl keeps me awake nights. What a disgrace! How am I going to tell her father? She is barely a child. If my sister, may she rest in peace, came back to life, she would die again of shame...This is horrible!..."cried the Pimentel woman.

Holding onto a chair to prevent herself from falling, Merceditas was white as a sheet. She could hardly speak a word.

"My son is a child, a kid without experience..."

"Oh, yeah?" exploded Pimentel with flaming eyes. "He was not a kid to do what he did. Whom did my niece get pregnant by, pray?"

The wedding was hastily arranged to protect the family good name. That was the right thing to do, avowed Merceditas, and my son always does the right thing, like the Valladares knights...

The most urgent task was to find a job for Juanjo.

"Look what your son's real artistic talents were!," reproached Celso. "It was all for nothing. If he had a career as I had said. But no. I am a nobody in my own house."

Merceditas kept silent, lacking the strength to respond. She was crushed by the whole mess. It was such a hard, unexpected blow that she hadn't reacted yet. She fell into total apathy. Not even the wedding arrangements: the ceremony, the clothes, the presents, all that in normal circumstances would have reconciled her to the fact, could snap her out of her indifference. Seeing her so listless worried her husband. Not only he stopped berating her, but he even tried to feign the opposite to his own feelings.

"But Merceditas, I have never seen you like this, so depressed...Cheer up! After all it isn't so bad. An illness, for instance, would have been worse," he tried to up and encourage himself. "Of course he is too young to be married; he should have grown up first, secure some position for himself...but it was bound to happen some time and you'd have to give him up. And think of your little grandson! You'll be the youngest grandmother of all..."

Nothing. She remained unmoved.

After pulling some strings, Juanjo was given a job at the local bank.

"I also started low, even worse than him, for I was a bellboy. And here I am," said the bank manager to Celso. "Here he can go far if he wants to. But of course, he has to do his part," and he volunteered some confidential advice on the best way to go to make himself agreeable and win his superiors over.

Celso could not imagine Juanjo that way. He had to be warned. He had to settle down. He was going to be a family man and that meant responsibility.

So many projects, so many dreams to have her son turn into an office boy! complained Merceditas to herself. Her anguish was so great that even Saint Xil was forgotten. Maybe she preferred not to remember him, considering the saints' betrayal allowing her defeat. Her life had been undone overnight. She had the impression that a catastrophe, a sweeping tornado had destroyed her home, her sanity, her happiness. Without him, Juanjo, her life was worthless. In desolation, she avoided her son, refusing even to look at him. She was afraid he could read the truth in her eyes. She was unable to control or subdue her overpowering emotions. Like impatient messages, her eyes would unwillingly gush forth passionate rays. She could not renounce the happiness built day by day in the intimacy of their talks, the complicity of their games. What gnawed at her heart the most was the conviction that no woman could ever take her place. The universe created by Juanjo and her could never be rebuilt by another woman. Even then Merceditas had the premonition that nobody could replace her. Juanjo could never find her likeness in the world. This certainly deepened her pain. All that destroyed, like that, she mumbled desperately, because of a single bad moment. It was all the fault of that flibbertygibbet, were it that she had never shown her face here...She had stolen him from her. Merceditas thought she would die of grief.

She lost a lot of weight. Dressed in black, in her matron of honor lace mantilla, she looked like a *mater dolorosa*. During the wedding ceremony her lace handkerchief was soaked with tears. Next to her,

Juanjo exquisitely pale, hardly noticed anything. He was so bewildered that someone had to help his trembling hand to slip the wedding band on the bride's finger. The girl, most serene in her role, looked more than ever a princess in her sober moiré silk wedding dress with its wide skirt. The family pearls, a gift from Aunt Pimentel, enhanced her round neck. An orange blossom, laying on her pew, testified of the purity of the bride. Next to her, her French diplomat father wore his tails as casually as a dressing gown, he being the only person who seemed to understand what the ceremony was all about.

The event went on at the high altar, without the main characters being aware of the gossiping of the guests.

"Merceditas has aged several years. She looks awful."

"I bet you anything the Frenchie has something in the oven. Otherwise, why the hurry to marry?"

"Well, look, she looks absolutely virginal."

"You'll see. These foreign girls, even those brought up by nuns...well, they are all fast ones."

"That man next to the Pimentel woman, the one with white sideburns is the French consul, one of the witnesses."

"Her father is a diplomat, isn't he? He looks really spiffy."

"No, but we have here la crème de la crème."

"What else?"

"Alvaro Xil gave them a valuable painting...I can't remember the painter's name..."

"A waste of time. It looks to me like the baby's already been ordered."

"Time will tell."

Only the birth of her grand child reconciled Merceditas with life. During the previous months she had seen her son rarely. She avoided him. She walked around the house like a lost soul. While knitting booties and little jackets she held on to her memories more than ever. Her husband did what he could to make her react but to no avail.

The baby was born in spring, and life started anew for Merceditas. She came to terms with her son, and a new lease on life began for her. He was divine, a sweet, hairless baby, and so perfect...

"Just like his father. He is precious!" said a friend.

"Not at all! He has his mother's mouth," said another.

Merceditas glared at her.

"He looks just like my Juanjo when he was born," asserted the new grandmother. "It seems to me I'm reliving those times. I feel the same emotion. My beautiful roly-poly baby!" she cried, pressing him against her breast.

Merceditas even decided the baby's name. Xil. He had to be called Xil like our saint. Thus he would ensure his protection for life.

The matter was not quickly settled. Araceli, his mother, wanted to call him René.

"Does your mother have to dictate also my son's name?"

"No, honey," replied Juanjo conciliatory. "But René is so French, so bland..."

"Well, that Xil, if he ever existed, was a Portuguese, another foreigner," objected Araceli.

"It is hardly the same thing. Besides he is our ancestor. And please, don't tell Mama he never existed. We might get in trouble..."

They came to an agreement. The baby would be called Xil René. His mother would call him always René, rolling the r's widely. For Merceditas he was just Xil. Very diplomatically Juanjo opted for not calling him anything. "Where is the king of the house?," he would coo approaching the baby's cradle.

Since Araceli was so busy with the baby, Juanjo started seeing his friends again. first at the "Madrid" café for afternoon coffee. Then, in the evenings, for wine. Afterwards came suppers. He was hardly ever home. After the whirlwind courtship of that summer, Araceli no longer attracted him. She was like a trophy, put aside once won. Maternity had ripened her beauty; she looked sweet and delicate as a Florentine madonna. But Juanjo would rather look at her than touch her, as if holding her close would break the spell of her miraculous beauty. They hardly had sex anymore. First it was her pregnancy. Then the birth, since the delivery stitches made sexual contact painful. Afterwards it was the baby's crying at night...With the excuse that he had to get up early in the morning he moved out of the bedroom.

If wily Merceditas, anticipating her son's matrimonial failure, had thought she would get him back, she was disappointed. Juanjo would never return to the old games in his mother's sitting room. His aroused instincts required other kind of games. Whatever had burned was now extinguished.

Carefree Juanjo would not miss any gathering or festive occasion. Always carousing; today to eat trout at Bieito's, whose wife prepared trouts like no one in the world: with that picante paprika which made them so tasty...To be fully enjoyed, trouts must have seven f's: freezing, fresh-served, free, full, flexible and female. Bieito would wink his eye at the remaining f-word. The Chantada's red wine took care of the rest. Tomorrow it would be puff pastries at Neno's. Saturday, foreleg ham... everywhere. Like the hornpiper at village feasts Juanjo was. As the neighbors would gossip, if you don't do it when single, you'll do it when married. His wit and friendliness attracted everybody. Miguel Anxo, a slim dark young man in tapered pants, blue polo shirt and a sweater knotted around the hips, could not tear himself away from him.

They used to go on outings. Particularly in the summertime they didn't miss a single festivity in the region. In Lugo they felt suffocated. There was nowhere to dance, to listen to music...Nothing. Only bars and taverns. Lots of food and no more. The towns on the seacoast where somewhat far but they turned out to be more fun.

"How different in temper are these seaports!" commented Chuco.

"There is a different typology between sea people and inlanders," said a know-it-all from Vivero, a student in Santiago University. "Inlanders are close, conservative. People on the coast are more open-minded. The ocean widens your worldview. Upon the shore, sailors spend all the money they have without care. They sing, shout, and give themselves to life because they are used to risk it with every tide."

"Basically they are more generous, and their sense of property is different, right?" replied Juanjo.

"The reason is simple," hastens to reply the expert knowingly. "The ocean belongs to everybody; the land is my own. Peasants can start a fistfight for an inch of land. Their whole life is spent in litigation. The borders, the feet, the markers, the water...Eternal discord, sickle in hand."

"Yes, now that you mention it, it's curious. They always carry their sickle, even
going for a walk."

"They argue that a bramble, a snake, or a branch on the path may require cutting away...but in reality it's a threat," insisted the man from Vivero." "People should talk and understand each other, shouldn't they, Mr. So-and-So?' says the peasant woman, her body posed forward while twiddling her sickle."

"Look at them!" said Miguel Anxo. "Will it be for that reason that the sickle is considered a revolutionary symbol, and that's why the Communists adopted it as their emblem?"

"The hammer also. And I've never seen a carpenter walking around carrying it in his hand."

"The sickle is more appropriate," said Juanjo. "Even before that. Notice that Death is usually portrayed ready to reap severed heads."

"It must be that picture that makes you see peasant women so fierce. My grandmother uses the sickle in her work, poor thing, and she is a peaceful soul incapable of hurting a fly. You are a bunch of babblers..."

They wasted little time on these considerations. They enjoyed their revelries in seaside haunts, eating octopus and clams, listening to the habaneras sung by their boisterous patrons. 'Don't mind the boat, don't mind the capsized boat. I mind the pilot, mind the lost pilot and the lost crew' they sang, heads laid back, eyes locked on each other, holding on to their starry gazes as if not to fade away into alcoholic oblivion.

That day would remain engraved on fire in Juanjo's mind. Who would have thought it, seeing him among the carousers, drinking and singing...But that day something was in the air, the way dogs feel approaching death. And on he went, still water in readiness, to fall into the pit. It was written.

They were coming back from Foz in Chuco's Seat 600. Juanjo sat in the back with Miguel Anxo. They were singing 'Only you.' Miguel Anxo stared fixedly into his eyes the way the sailors of the tavern had done. When the song was finished, Juanjo felt the other's breathing close, his mesmerizing eyes burning into his. He felt his hand first on his knee, then going up confidently towards his inner thigh till resting on his soft genitals.

Juanjo never forgot that moment. It was as if celestial trumpets sounded, and heaven burst into bright, golden clouds. None of the experiences he would later have in life could match the joy felt under that boyish hand. The initial surprise of the unexpected action gave way immediately to enormous anxiety. When reflecting on the moment afterwards, his clearest thought was his quick acceptance of the situation as if it were the most natural thing in the world, a normal occurrence. Body attraction is simple or would be, were it not for those who idealize, overcomplicate things, building barriers or taboos. Juanjo enjoyed his pleasure without embarrassment or care. He pressed his hand over Miguel Anxo's while feeling his previous softness grow harder and bigger. He suppressed a cry behind his partner shoulder. The driver protested:

"How come you are so quiet back there?...You are not asleep, are you? Come on, wake up. We still have twenty kilometers to go, and I'll fall asleep too if you don't sing. Look at this bugger, how he snores," he pointed at his companion, asleep by his side.

The kilometers till Lugo went by for Juanjo as in a mist. Dazed on a delightful trance he never knew how he was finally able to remove himself from Miguel Anxo's sight or to go up the stairs of his home. He opened the door absently, almost surprised that the key turned, and walked the hallway as if for the first time. He stared at his sleeping wife as if she were a stranger. Slowly he approached his son's cradle. The serenity of that little china doll face, his soft breathing, the sweetness of childhood sleep contrasted his own turmoil. It seemed as if the placidity of the infant disapproved of his disorderly conduct. He felt tears rolling down his cheeks. A teardrop hit the baby's pink cheek and he began to stir, as if about to cry. Juanjo escaped the room like a thief, fearing being surprised by mother and son.

He could not sleep that night. He went to work in a dream after excusing himself with Araceli. It's alright, I don't want any coffee. I'll breakfast out, and he bolted avoiding her eyes and her resentment.

The morning was an eternity. At the bank, he misplaced cheques, had to count the money three times in a row...Come on, Viéitez! reproved the manager when Juanjo presented him the wrong form to sign.

When leaving through the door he was sure to find him, and so it was. There was Miguel Anxo, with white ultra narrow pants and a blue Lacoste polo shirt. They started to walk. Eagerly they entered an apartment building and kissed passionately in the hallway behind the main door. Juanjo felt the other's bitter and aggressive tongue in his mouth, his strong legs against his; the hard penis slashing his thighs; his daring, almost brutal hands crushing his own hardness. It was a savage attack, an unknown passion, vastly different from Juanjo's former experience. With Araceli it was a shy entanglement, a tender encounter. They arrived to intercourse like a prank, after having looked at each other for a long time, caressing slowly, kissing softly on the lips. Even in the most passionate moments he was careful not to hurt her, not to crush her under his weight. He was almost grateful she hadn't been a virgin, sparing him having to tear her up, to make her bleed. The short relationship with Araceli was child's play compared to this fury. He felt adult, strong, complete.

An opening door in one of the apartments and approaching footsteps compelled them to leave. Deftly Miguel Anxo knotted his sweater to his waist to hide the telling stains in front of his pants. Juanjo put his coat on. The situation made them burst into conspiratorial laughter. They laughed openly, feeling the tension happily leaving their bodies.

A new life began for Juanjo. He considered himself grown up, made. What attracted him the most of making love to a man was the merciless clash with another body, the unyielding manly strength, the rigorous and vehement, almost prickly caresses. He admired that virile roughness so different from female fragility. He was excited by the contact of a body like his own, knowing, ready to match his impulses, noticing his waves before they broke on the beach, guessing the moment where senses vanished like mist before the sun, that blinding sun of pleasure that carried them in triumph to the inevitable beach. His own potency was similar to his partner's, as evident the desire, as physical the excitement. He finally had a worthy opponent for the sexual battlefield, a challenger to the strength and dexterity of his sword in those sexual tournaments fit only for the brave born, and for those of superior intellect. It was a fight among equals, the pleasure of the likeness.

In exchange, to penetrate a woman was abuse, almost a crime, thought Juanjo. But also in time, a big snare. The female body, so pliable, did not oppose resistance and tore up like a loaf of bread, in a ripping holocaust. Only a sadistic could enjoy such possession. Or the frustrated ones, believing to have underneath a subjugated world offered to them by the surrendering woman in the form of slaughtered flesh. It was an illusion, and men fell into the trap. In the end, it was men themselves who were imprisoned in the hole...Women's holes served so many purposes...When he entered Araceli he could not stop thinking that he had come out of a similar hole himself. The mother was always present. Men, he liked to think at that time, poor puppets! We come from a hole, and we spend our lives crazy to crawl back in. The thing is never to be free from Mother. Go to sleep, my baby...tenderness upon tenderness over female laps. On intercourse, the advancing penis entered the womb, the baby's first cradle, walking to the not-to-be, to death by pleasure. We go back to where we were, to the origin, our former country. We get lost in the abyss, reaching nothingness, and we come back to life to be delivered anew by our mothers. When we spring out the penis we become men again. Some modern husbands called their wives Mama. That's right, agreed Juanjo, all should call Mama the woman they are sleeping with. Mama!, before entering their body; Mama!, hold me tight; Mama!, let me snuggle up to you...Always Mama.

Not now for him. He was cutting off the cord, setting himself free of Mama, of all Mamas, of their spell, their fake weaknesses, their honeyed flatteries, the slimy quicksand, the sucking hole. Now he was a man near men; he finally had found his own likeness.

After some time Juanjo could not understand how his marriage could still last in those circumstances. Araceli was too weak to confront him or to leave. She kept silent. Her family and all the others weighed heavily on her. Her hasty wedding, thought the girl, had been shocking enough...Now she could not part from her husband. She could not start another upheaval. Besides, what could she allege? That Juanjo was never home? That was normal. Home is not a man's world. People saw them on Sundays, strolling with the baby, drinking vermouth at the "Terrace" before going to Merceditas' or to her aunt's for lunch. Juanjo, charming as ever, so loving, drawing a chair for her; what would you drink?; playing with the baby, full of patience...a doting father! The baby, ungrateful brat, complained Araceli, as soon as his father appeared would go crazy, running into his arms, Papa, Papa!; din, don, din don, Juanjo would dandle him, or carried him piggyback while the little beast hollered with laughter. People looked at them approvingly. What a family scene! Araceli gnashed her teeth. The kid was crazy about his father. Juanjo was a visitor in his own home, but the less time he spent with him, the more the baby loved him. As soon as his father showed up, he wouldn't even look a her, the one who put up with him at all times, and was bringing him up practically alone.

On her part, Merceditas was squaring accounts with that hypocrite who had stolen her son from her. She could not share with anyone, not even Celso, her satisfaction on the failure of that marriage. She did not spare any opportunity to remind Araceli, albeit diplomatically, of course. Leave Xil with me any time you want to go out with Juanjo. Let him even sleep over, so that you don't have to worry about time. I'll be delighted, you know...she let her words down softly like a tinker bell. That bitch knows very well Juanjo never takes me anywhere, thought Araceli while answering, no, thank you very much, but you know I am not at ease; he is so young yet...The baby was a pretext for her reclusion. He was also her only reason to live. However, after the few first months when her son needed her the most, maternity's first joys began to fade. Araceli wallowed in solitude. Hungry for other needs and feelings she took refuge in her child. She watched him grow in fear because, as the baby became older, he was more independent, and she felt less needed.

The emptiness of her life became obvious to her. Where was that much touted about marriage bliss? Frustration and helplessness gnawed at her heart, souring her temper. She was silent: whom would she talk to? She didn't dare to confide in anyone. She was ashamed of her failure, she the winner, the little princess. Sometimes she imagined that it hadn't happened, that she was home in Paris, the life of the party, greeting her friends charmingly...They would all have finished high school by now, maybe college. And there she was, trapped at the other side of the world, shrouded in mist...Black thoughts engulfed her. Would it be like this till the end of her life? Her son would keep growing while she withered in that walled town like a plant without water. Every night she had the same dream. She would go effortlessly up a long staircase till she reached the summit of an immense mountain from where she could see open spaces extending to the rosy horizon. A gentle breeze caressed her face. She would laugh and laugh while stretching her arms forward. Laughter turned into tears when she woke up and remembered the dream. She was suffocating in her home prison. Outside she was like an autumn leaf. She was nothing or maybe just Juanjo's wife. But she actually knew she was not his wife at all. She had scribbled a few letters to her father about the situation, tearing them up afterwards. She didn't dare send them, afraid of being blamed for her unhappiness. If her mother were alive...She missed her more than ever. A bosom to take refuge on, to cry over, to unburden her grief into.

It was not Araceli's decision what changed things. It was scandal.

The parents of Chinto, a new friend of Juanjo's, had gone away to Sarria for the weekend, and the young men had the house to themselves. Chinto had a Kolster record player, and Saturday's prospects looked bright. Fate will let go agley the best laid plans. Chinto's mother sprained her ankle, breaking the ligaments, and had to be brought back home. With the Beatles in full blast, they couldn't hear anything. They were caught red-handed in the act.

"I wish I had broken both legs rather than this!" cried Chinto's mother weeping uncontrollably.

"Poor child!" Aunt Pimentel was sad for her niece. "I wish she had never come here. That good for nothing maricón, making her pregnant first and then...What rotten luck, sweet Jesus!"

Juanjo's parents, bewildered, watched Pimentel's overwhelming rage.

"And now what?" she inquired with flaming eyes. "This poor girl's life destroyed, and she still so young..."

Too young, Merceditas fought the rejoinder. If my son had found a proper woman he would never have done a thing like that. If his wife knew how to satisfy him...But these precious trinkets, kept in cotton wool...They are just paper dolls. Juanjo needed something else.

Araceli's father inevitably appeared.

"Now, now, babe, don't cry," he said reassuringly. "Nothing happened. We shall go home. Get ready. We are leaving, yes, we are leaving tomorrow."

"What about the baby?" cried Merceditas horrified when she found out. "She cannot take him away from us, just like that..."

"Of course she can, dear madam," pointed out the father firmly. "But you can keep him."

"Papa!" wailed Araceli. "He is my son!"

"Let me do, darling," replied her father firmly. "You have to get organized first, go back to school, straighten out you life...At this time you cannot be saddled with a baby. We'll see about that later."

Araceli would never set foot in that misty town again.

"We shall take care of your son," said Celso Viéitez to Juanjo. "As for you"—and his unusually raised voice trembled—"you'll never tread these boards again. That's for sure. You have dishonored the family name," he finished with his voice definitely broken and tears in his eyes. "You are not my son. You are not even a man."

Chapter 3

After the scandal blew over, Juanjo's imbroglio was put to rest. The affair never went beyond town gossip.

"They say that Merceditas' son is...like that, you know," insinuated someone making queer-like gestures.

"You don't say! I can't believe it! He is not the type..."

"His wife, the Frenchie, left him. It seems that when she came home she caught him in bed with 'Setetroitas' son, making out."

"Jesu!" cried the other crossing herself. "Just hearsay. People are so mean! So bad!...If one is not careful they'll tear you to shreds..."

"Look, honey, where there is smoke there is..."

"Well, I'm not saying it can't be true. It's just that I can't figure... He was always so sturdy, so mischievous..."

The matter faded into obscurity.

His father was the only one who couldn't forget. It was a blow to him. Shameful! he would lament. We shall never be able to wash the stain, even with holy water. Not daring to face the "Syphon" he stopped going to the tertulia. He thought it polite to make himself scarce. He could only imagine the badinage about such a cataclysmic occurrence. He couldn't do that to his friends. They would be so happy feasting on the tasty scraps; they were specially good at it. Who could face them! They would show no mercy, Celso Viéitez kept thinking while he walked aimlessly around the town, oblivious of the rain soaking his serge suit. Figueroa would even make up one of his satirical ditties. He could even listen to it: "Troubadour ancestors, maricón descendants...," or something similar.

He was not thick-skinned enough to bear with it.

But Celso was wrong about his friends. Juanjo's peccadillo flew away like a sparrow in the wind, even at the "Syphon."

"It is just gossip..."

"Sure. There is no evidence..."

"He is Celso's son, not just anybody's..."

"The subject is complicated, I mean, it is sensitive..."

With phrases like these the matter was put to rest. The "Syphon" members, always looking for tidbits and petty chitchat to vent their spleen on, were well-behaved this time.

At home, Celso remained silent. He never wanted to hear from his son again. He told his wife he would rather see him dead, and that was all. He was never talkative, but Juanjo's affair made him even more taciturn. He mumbled all the insults he would not say aloud. He kept moping around the streets, avoiding places where he could meet acquaintances. Most of all he shunned the Plaza Mayor, of course, the people's living room, as Pimentel called it, and hid under the arches of Campo square, where he could always duck, although immersed in his thoughts he was not likely to notice anybody. Mumbling strange words, he would go down Miño street, diving dangerously into the miserable alleys of Lugos's underworld. He favored the redlight district where, like in every city, bad women were easy to find. Who would say that wherever poverty, misery and filth abounded, the so-called pleasure houses were to be found! Nobody knew why, since what satisfaction, gaiety, pleasurable or joyful sensations could anybody find amidst such disgusting indignity? But Celso never thought of this, ruminating aimlessly on his problem. When he noticed something—the smell of poverty, the looks of certain women standing on the threshold of their huts—he escaped in haste, as quick as his dignity and pride would allow. He was afraid that someone would recognize him. A pervert son was enough; it didn't need a whoring father also. Saint Xil!, he cried, imitating his wife.

As best she could, Merceditas never stopped communicating with Juanjo. She sent him messages, met him secretly, careful that Celso would not find out. He was so furious, she would tell Juanjo, that he would kick her out of the house too...Saint Xil! She had never seen him like that. Such a peaceful man, and now, so enraged...It didn't seem true.

The furtive encounters renewed the intimacy between mother and son. They enlivened wily Merceditas' imagination. "I'll wait for you at eight at the Virgin of the Big Eyes," the note said. Juanjo entered the Cathedral, went to the right chapel and saw his mother, kneeling in front of Our Lady with a pious attitude, her moist eyes contrasting the statue's empty gaze, those big eyes for which it was known. Our Lady's remoteness matched Merceditas' absent mind. Her heart was elsewhere in the same way Our Lady was oblivious of the baby clinging to her bosom, ignoring the claim of the little hand on her breast, an absent breast that not even the lively little angels flitting around could make alive. Like the statue, Merceditas was far away, her heart a-fluttering.

I am sure she's not praying, thought Juanjo who knew her well. She feels my presence. She is so excited by the waiting, the date, the whole setup, she can't pray. She is enjoying all this, deep inside she relishes it. Juanjo played her game and brushed past her without stopping. She noticed him immediately...His step, his smell...She turned around, surreptitiously. She looked at him and her eyebrows rose. Her eloquent eyes gave him directions. She crossed herself, rose and went towards a dark corner, behind a column. There they talked in whispers. Before leaving she would put a small parcel in his hand. A piece of pork empanada I made today. I know you love it...This piece of cake for lunch, sweet tooth...Here, cream cookies, although some of them got a little burnt because Xil was making mischief in my bedroom, and when I realized it...He surely is a scamp.

In time she made their dates more and more complicated. At dark, in that recess of the wall by Santiago's gate, remember? she would say dreamily. She imagined Juanjo appearing on horseback, so sure of himself, picking her up airily to carry her pillion, herself holding on tight to his waist lest she fall. With throbbing heart she would feel not the horse's strength but her son's...till they arrived to a copse or hidden grove—where would Crecente's lay?—where they could talk at length.

Once she even made him get into a confessional. At that time Father Ruibal was away, asserted Merceditas. Hail Mary, most pure, she would announce kneeling down and feeling his breath close to hers. She would tell him about her life. She reminisced on old times games, the medieval poets, her dreams of her son's brilliant acting career. She hoped to soften his father's stance to allow him to return home and continue the rehearsals...You are not going to spend your life at that bank, my son. To act out the game, the son dictated her penance. My child, repent your sins and pray a Salve to our Lady and five...What? Merceditas ruffled her feathers. Putting up with your father who, since your business happened is behaving like a devil...He is totally unbearable. And then taking care of Xil, a naughty brat who is driving me crazy...

She would tell her son things she would not confess to a priest.

Juanjo went along with the dating game so as not to disappoint her. She had suffered enough as it was. But he did not enjoy the fantasies as before. He made an effort to show an enthusiasm he hardly felt. On the other hand, for her, the old passion rekindled like a strong, well fed flame. Sometimes, in the middle of the winter, the dark corners proposed by Merceditas for the encounter were ice cold. She didn't seem to mind. Let's go into a café, suggested Juanjo, frozen. What? If your brute of a father finds out we are seeing each other...Saint Xil! it gives me the creeps just to imagine it. He is getting suspicious, though...I swear my heart stops at the thought! After this she changed her tune and the initial terror gave way to self–pity. I am worried, she went on, about your father. He used to be a big trenchman...but now he just picks at his food. Soon he will be as thin as a rail. Aie, son! I have to go on like this because he is...Like going crazy. One day he'll become like Sun Worshipper, I'm telling you...

Sun Worshipper was a poor crazy beggar roaming the Lugo streets in a threadbare black suit. Kneeling on the ground, and always facing the sun, the staple of his madness, he worshipped. When Juanjo was a kid and saw Sun Worshipper by Cantón Lane so piously engaged, he believed he was praying to Saint Xil. Not wasting any opportunity to raise the status of the family saint, Merceditas let him believe it. And now, Merceditas was seeing her own husband, his mind already lost, going around Lugo's streets the way of that poor madman.

Time heals. Merceditas wiles were more convincing and warmer than the sun's, and Celso Viéitez finally came back to himself. He even returned to the 'Syphon' where he was received by his friends without constraint. All things seemed to go back to normal except Merceditas' hopes of getting her son back. Juanjo's new sexual orientation had made her hopeful. Deep inside she went along with her sons's homosexuality because it meant she was the woman, the only woman in his life. Other men, Juanjo's possible lovers, were not her rivals. She could not be jealous of those anomalies. They were but games, superficial attachments, nothing comparable to the depth of their feelings, the perfect identification between them, their understanding, their likeness.

Alien to his mother's illusions, Juanjo was building his nest. He rented an attic. There was no elevator but luckily his friends had lent a hand with the moving and the decoration of the place. So that he lacked nothing they even got him a bitch, a Carny no less.

"You with a dog!" said Merceditas. "You'll be like Xulia Minguillón who is crazy about her dog, and even cries for him. What a sight you'll be, always with your bag of treats for the mutt!"

"You can't compare," protested Juanjo. "This is a pedigree dog, not a mongrel. A Valladares cannot own just any dog," he concluded observing his mother's expression when he mentioned the family pride.

"But son," she argued, "in that shoebox where you live, where shall you put it?"

Little did she know how accommodating Juanjo's niche would come to be.

"Grandpa," said Xil René upon coming home, "you should see my dad's dog...It's a purebred. Her name is Rosiña."

"Rosiña?" Celso made a wry face. "What a name! It's a bitch, I suppose."

"No, grandpa. It's a dog," affirmed the kid, puzzled by his grandfather's subsequent reaction of leaving the room after slamming the door.

Juanjo decorated his apartment with the help of a window dresser friend, a true expert on those matters.

"I want a canopied bed. Yes, like zat. And I want mauve veils, lotsss of gauze hangers," requested Juanjo in his new affected speech. "In the living room, plenty of pillowsss; here, there, on the corner, all real cozy, huh? It is all so preciousss!" he exclaimed joining his hands as in prayer. "The housewarming party will be an aux chandelles dinner."

Thus the apartment began to take shape, a mixture of Madame Pompadour's drawing room and a cocotte's meublé.

After confiding in some of his Lugo friends, he formed a new, different group in town. They stood out in the insouciance of their conduct, and their sartorial prowess. They were the smart set. Juanjo looked always perfectly accessorized. Black pants that elongated his figure; black patent leather shoes, black belt of the same material. As a contrast, yellow sweater and socks. Black sunglasses would complete his outfit. Le rouge et le noir, he would say aloud to himself, looking pleased at the mirror before going out. He had his father's figure and stance. But his father was a classical dresser whereas Juanjo was inclined to extravagance. When having coffee at the 'Cantón Bar' and the 'Monterrey' or drinks at the 'Piper's,' Juanjo and his friends were a sensation.

He spent many weekends away from Lugo, making friends in all the towns he visited. He knew how to mingle and single out the people of the hood. His naturally gregarious personality, his aplomb, and his appearance, even more outlandish outside Lugo, made connections easy for him. Juanjo could not go anywhere unnoticed.

He decided to give a party at home inviting his friends from out of town. It was a success. More parties followed. One thing led to another, and thanks to Juanjo all homosexuals of the area came together. Lugo became the Mecca of the hood, and Juanjo's little apartment, as if it were made out of rubber, stretched out to admit people from all corners of Galicia.

Juanjo took care of the happenings with grace and good sense. With the help of a friend or two he started Friday getting ready for the party. All details had to be taken care of. Beverages, appetizers, canapés should be aplenty. On Saturday afternoon, the preparations complete, Juanjo made his personal toilette with the same care. Bathing salts, a net to tame his curly hair, eyeshadow...He was now ready to welcome his guests. Early evening the doorbell rang, and the all-night show began. The apartment door became the curtain. After crossing the threshold the adlib but customary comedy lasted as long as the players could bear. Sometimes it even ended in drama. There was no particular genre or script but they all knew the performance would be closer to a Valle-Inclán esperpento than to the melancholic restraint of a Chekhov's play. Among the excessive cries and kisses, the outlandish animation and speech, there was only a mandatory rule in that hullabaloo: the nonstop teasing and humor the players squeezed out of their wits.

Curtain was up as the doorbell rang.

"Hellooo!" cried old queer Naparreto Jarsía coming in. "Oh, baby, you live in the world's asshole!"

"How explicit, honey," greeted Juanjo. "Yours is an obsession."

"Oh, yesss!, he nodded, his chin going mechanically up and down his chest the way of those toy car-dogs that move their heads with the car's motion. "I can't figure how the Romans stumbled into this place. And what a chore, baby, that big, big wall!"

"Aie! What a hole!" hooted Moor-Eater Lili, plopping down into the cushions after the long stair climb. "I am pooped! Let me collapssse on these cushions. How sssoft! We can share them, right sweeties? Ufff!" he sighed loudly spreading his arms, "I feel like sprawling. SSprawling!"

"We'll call you Couching Lili," teased Juanjo when he saw him lying down among the pillows.

"Oh, no, no, no!" he replied bringing down his arm halfway in an arc like a dancer and stopping like an unwound doll. "The crunching reminds me of Christmas nougat. It makes me blue."

Juanjo had a knack for calling names. No one was free of his chafings, but even the victims laughed at his clever, witty barbs.

"See how you find me!" said the host to a new guest, a brawny dark man whose full mouth was set off by lipstick.

"French corduroy, girls," strutted around Flaky Olga.

"Here blows in Lucia of Lammermoor!" somebody heralded at the door spoiling Olga's parade.

"Lucia blows what?," he asked rather peeved.

A fat queen appeared, jerking his arms and ponderously swaying his hips as if he wore crinoline. He greeted his host formally, gasping for breath after the long climb. He exhaled deeply.

"Good evening, Widow Roquefort." That was Juanjo's pet name for himself in memory of the French woman. "I have prepared an aria to delight you. Ah, ah, ah!" he warbled with his husky voice.

"Here, drrink up and get your voice in shape," offered Naparreto Jarsía, the Rías Baixas fop. "We'll make a duet later."

"I suspect that our styles differ...but we can try. Let's see"—and he reached out for Navarrete's bulge.

"Oh, how booold! These opera divas are...well they always want to call the music. Have a drrink first," he navigated as slippery as a fish testing the waters.

"What are you drinking?" asked Sassy Purita to Moor eater Lili sipping from his glass. "Ugh, how ssweet!"

"Oh yes, sweet, sweet, sweet. Just like me, baby. My kisses are famous, didn't y'know? Like Cointreau and pineapple."

"I'd rather have a big banana," said Purita rolling his eyes.

"Who is the one by the door, lonely and pale, with a drink in her hand?" asked Nijinsky Spread-Legs to his neighbor.

"Oh, zat one! It's Whispering Pines. She always looks languid. Never says a word but she misses nothing. She is crazy about Juanjo," explains Asuction Sagasta.

"What a sack! Aie! I'll stay, I'll stay, I'll stay," crooned Spread-Legs lying down on Juanjo's bed, holding his raised leg with his hand like a ballet dancer. "Like disss, among the veilss...What a dance, baby!"

"And you, with that scarf around your neck?" Juanjo greeted a newcomer. "Hush, don't tell me, don't tell me. It's mumps, isn't it?" He changed his tone and commiserated: "That's the limit," he dramatized rising his arms. "What if you became barren? Saint Xil forbid! I want your baby!" he hammed falling at the feet of a tall dark–eyed, long–lashed blond with a scarf knotted round the neck.

"Be quiet, be quiet," answered Peroxide María, his opponent. "You don't know what happened...Look!" he dramatically removed the scarf showing his neck all blue.

"Boy, what a hickey! What a banquet, girls! A night with Dracula, of course," laughed Juanjo.

"Don't be silly," interrupted the man waving his hand down slowly. "Have you met the Tropicana, that eye doctor from A Coruña?," and he clucks his tongue in his mouth as if tasting a delicacy. "I ran into him at Porches. Would you like a drink? Alright, I said. He looked smashing, as usual. So exuberant! All of us are crazy about him. He looked at me with those trropical eyes, you know, deeep. Latin Americans look differently, right?"

"So what?" cut in Shameless Doris who had been eavesdropping. "Honey, how you drivel!"

"Well," he clucked his tongue again, "he asked me: Shall we go to my place? What digss! He has a chalet. Preciouss! With a fireplace." His tone changed. "But would you believe? Not a drink. Not even the petting couch. Straight to the bedroom. A rococo bed with a fur bedspread...furs on the floor...Aie! What could I tell you, my dears? A dream! What a night, I thought. Well, take your clothes off, he ordered me drily. And I, a little miffed, started to strip. He took everything off in a shot," he clucked his tongue. "And I who enjoys foreplay so much!...But he got on top of me soo fast! Right on the target, you know. And I said no and no. I didn't like it that way as if I were a common whore. And besides he was soo big! Enormous!" he chuckled. "Well, I managed to turn around and told him no, that I didn't care for it at all, damn it! Then he started sucking on my neck...I thought he was getting soft," he blinked innocently among the listeners' guffaws. "When I saw myself in the mirror like this—"he pointed to his neck—"Oh my! How can I show myself in public? I applied vinegar, icepacks...everything. What a pig! It'a a real bummer."

"Aie!" cried Asuction startled when he saw the dog. "What is disss? How ssweet!" he crooned looking at the spruced up dog's earrings, necklace, big pink bow on the head and tiny pink lace briefs.

"It's Rosiña," pointed Whispering Pines softly."

"Rosiña, poochie, poochie," he called to make her come over. "She is cute. And she doesn't object to wearing all that?"

"Oh, no! She is used to it already. She wears such darling outfits!

Her Mama dresses her beautifully, doesn't she?" said Sassy giving the dog a piece of tortilla.

"Look who's here!" cried Juanjo batting his hands joyously as cymbals. "Sea-Breaker! Aie, what a sailor!! Striped sweater, navy pants...'He came on a boat, of a foreign name, I met him on the port...'," sang Juanjo in a falsetto voice, holding Breaker by the waist and dancing tango steps.

"He is doing his military service in the Navy," explained Whispering Pines peevishly to Naparreto.

"How is the crew?" asked Juanjo. "Very cocky, they tell me."

"What a chore, baby! In the showers everyone messing with everyone else. Shameless! It even made me, me!," he hit his breast with his palm, "blush. Yes, ssweeties, I was purple as a schoolgirl."

"A shrinking violet!" ironized Asuction Sagasta.

"They fondle each other like crazy. Even those who do not belong, do it...Imagine!" and he fluttered his hand like a seagull. "The first day, a mate told me: Shall we go to "Beirut" for a drink? Alright, let's go. So we went, and guess who was already there!" he paused, rolling his eyes and licking his lips as if tasting aromatic liqueur. "The skipper! Oh yeah! Brief," he paused and wetted his lips again, "he was devouring me with his eyes. And he kept sstaring, sstaring at me," he fixed his darkset eyelined gaze in the audience. "When we went back to the ship he asked me if I wanted to see his cabin. The sly one he didn't waste any time...And bang!, he ended abruptly. "The inevitable happened."

"What a blast! He looks so unworldly, yet his first sally is with the captain!" cried Shameless Doris her arms akimbo.

"Waaait! "Waait! Let me go on," protested Breaker silencing him with his hand. "Of course, darlings," and he feigned to taste an exquisite morsel, "I fell in love madly with my captain, quite lost my head over him. When we went to Marín, nothing but the best for me. I kept visiting his cabin. But when we returned to Ferrol, the picture changed. He had to see someone, had business somewhere...I had enough," he said drily, seeking approval from the audience. "I was to stay on board locked up. Sure! So I made myself up real cute in my whites...A doll! I went to town for a drink but didn't know anybody. All of a sudden it began to rain...and I in my whites and no umbrella. I ducked under a shop sign and looked at the window. Out of nowhere a convertible pulled over. I looked inside, and what a sight, girls! A real piece. Green eyes, blond mustache, aie!! What a hunk! Meanwhile I pretended to be interested in the parfums on the window. He came closer and asked: "Are you by yourself? What are you doing here? Well, as you see I was caught in the rain like diss," and he pointed up and down. "I'll give you a ride. Hop in. And I did," he rolled his tongue and looked at the other as if telling some feat. "Well...we went to a bar for a drink and while we were there whom do you think showed up? The skipper! Yes, and with a shit of a queer, a gigolo. And he stared and stared at us. He was furious, of course, seeing me with that hunk. What a surprise, you around here! Well, as you see. Then I told the other, Carlos was his name, shall we go? And we went to his place. Very ssmart, with walls full of paintings. He was from a very well known Santiago family, real classy," he paused lowering his eyelashes. "Well, then, bang! I was quite swept off my feet. We made a date for three days later. I was determined to jilt skipper forever but," he paused expectantly, "when I returned to the ship he was again all over me. Come here you fast one...and I avoiding him as much as I could. On the day I was to meet Carlos just upon leaving, where are you going? Out for a walk. Oh, yeah? Come here! He pushed me into his cabin. He threw my clothes off and there we go, out on a poke. Me protesting, I don't feel like it. Leave me. He was just a fucker, you know. No and no! Then you are not leaving here, he said locking up the room. What a bastard. He drilled in me all he wanted while I thought of the other, waiting. I cried my eyes out. Next day I went ashore but I didn't know where to find him...so I went to a movie theater and saw 'Butch Cassidy and the Sundance kid.'

"Those Navy men are all the same!" said Naparreto Jarsía. "Imagine. The other day I was out with a guy in "Pompom" in Santiago. He was rather grroovy, a little old fart but he looked promising...and he did deliver. He hadn't shaved and his face bristled a little which played havoc with my skin...but that was not the worst. Next day I feel an itchy itch...Couldn't stop scratching. And all of a sudden I discovered those white little crawlers..."

"The clap!" guffawed Juanjo. "You got crab lice, my boy. Of course with your size, what else could you get?

"Cut the shit out," protested Naparreto. "I never had anything like that, and I got scared. So I went to see Lacy Chelito."

"What a name," interrupted Marysilly. "She is a lace maker, right?"

"No, she is a male nurse, but she laces real well. She gave me some drink, ugh! Real grossss. I never wanted to see that Navy officer again.

I was sooo disgusted, sooo disgusted...I swear. I learned my lesson. No more seafarers."

They opened the balcony's doors and went out for a breath free from the crowd, alcohol and tobacco floating indoors.

Juanjo's apartment building stood near the police station. The merry guests went out in the balcony to make fun of the police officers standing guard by the door.

"Señora Widow Roquefort, come here!" cried Sassy gaily. "The police lieutenant down there said he is pining away for you and is coming right up!"

"My pleasure," agreed Juanjo. "Let him come! Let him come! But with his rod, right?"

All flocked to the balcony.

"Whoa!! What a dish!" someone cried from above.

"Aie, watch that one! I'll jump down to get him sooner," cried Shameless Doris.

"Come with me, window climber," called Juanjo to her.

They both went into the bathroom. Juanjo lowered his pants and sat on the toilet. He always urinated sitting down.

"Look Doris, honey, tell Pines or anybody to help you pick up things. Light the candles and prepare the stage for the show. You know...I have to put my makeup on..."

It was now time for the stage numbers. That never failed at Juanjo's parties. Already seasoned by his mother's theatrical performances, he always played the lead. He opened his closet to pick up the outfit. Let's see, the miniskirt...the long green silk...the yellow lace...That's it!

While he dressed he remembered his mother's bedroom and his fears of someone coming unexpectedly and catching him in drag, all made up...Now he wasn't afraid anymore. Of anything. He took the world in stride. People—who cares? Let them lighten up. We live no longer in the Inquisition.

"Watch out, Juanjo," warned Maruxa during their long walks together. "You are calling too much attention to yourself on the street. You are a loudmouth saying anything you like in front of anybody...You'll run into trouble one of these days."

Maruxa was his newest confident. She was tall, elegant and carefree. She had been away from Lugo studying for many years. She was free from provincial prejudice and did not mind being seen with Juanjo's notorious gang. She matched their exotism and sartorial prowess. Both

Juanjo and Maruxa looked like models out of a magazine.

"Quit, quit, quit" protested Juanjo. I don't give a fuck. So whaaat?" and he lifted his head with Valladares arrogance. "Besides, do I bother them? Do I rub their noses in their miseries, their shit? The way they trample on the people working for them? The way they cheat on their wives using poor starving whores? How can their laadies look down their noses at others when they are wearing fur coats obtained by submission and indignity?" observed Juanjo angrily. "They want difference within order. I want it within disorder. So the hell with them!"

"Hush! Don't shout," Maruxa tried to calm him down.

"How can you expect me not to shout! I wish I'd find a voice strong enough to pierce the walls that encircle and protect them, smoke out the caves where they hide, open the quaint tombs where they bury us, where they confine us. Can't you see I'm suffocating trying to keep up appearances?"

"One has to be discrete. It is wise not to look at the sun in the face; lest you die blind. All things must remain hidden, cool, softened by a shading veil."

"By hypocrisy, you mean. But the light of truth doesn't blind me. I am like a mirror, and they fear my reflection. Most of all they fear seeing themselves in it. That's why they avoid me. That's why they don't confront me. Society ladies, the bitches, look at you disapprovingly, but when you go and flatter them saying they don't look a year older, or how do they manage to look so well, not a wrinkle...They ruffle up like clucking hens and dissolve in smiles. This young man, whatever he may be, he is so charming, so polite. Of course, blood will tell. What a pity he is a...they sigh to their friends. And their husbands, the macho men, make wry faces when they encounter you in the street, looking disgusted, stuffed with dignity they do not have."

"Don't forget they make the rules," argued Maruxa. "They hold the reins..."

"They wish I reined them. Don't look at me like that. Their anger is the result of repression and envy. I can see it in the eyes of many of them. Haven't you noticed? They all react like cabrones. Even when they deny it, deep down they are all as maricones as we are. That's why they hate us. Can't you understand? Otherwise they would be indifferent to us. But no. They hate everything that exposes them, all things they refuse to accept about themselves."

"Yeah, yeah," Maruxa dismissed Juanjo's rethoric which seemed more and more a ranting and a raving. "More to the point. You must be careful in what you say and do. One of these days you'll be in for a fall and break your neck, my sweet."

"Bar the Evil Eye!" said Juanjo bending the two central fingers of his hand.

While he shaved, he thought of Maruxa's warning. After all, what did he have to lose? That shit of a job at the bank...Even slaves are permitted to be maricones. But he would never get ahead, for sure. He would never hold any important position. It looks like I've put on weight. I can't zip up. Now the high-heeled shoes. That was the worst part. It was a real bummer. With these big feet I can't find shoes that fit. What martyrdom, Saint-Xil! Beauty comes through suffering. Lots of white powder on his face. Yes, today I want to look pale, with rings under my eyes. False eyelashes on black lined eyes, a crimson mouth...A long black wig, ah! and a red feather in the hair...like this. Doris! he called going to the door with mincing steps.

"How do I look?" he asked turning around to be better seen.

"What a vamp!" admired Doris.

"Introduce me, will you?" said Juanjo picking up a fan from the drawer and opening it with a flourish, swinging his arm. It was hard for him to keep his balance with the heels and all the ingested alcohol.

"Here we are, darlings!" boomed Doris. "Let the Lugo Show begin. Heeeeeeere is the Widow Roquefort!"

Juanjo appeared swaying his hips, shaking the feather in his hair, fanning his face slowly, only his bewitching, dilated pupils in view of the audience. He veiled his eyes, lifting and lowering his fan while singing: 'I am by day a fire eagle, but just a woman at night...' with a hoarse, slightly off-key voice.

Needless to say the shows Juanjo put on were very different from the ones at his mother's. The audience couldn't care less about his ancestors, the brave knights, Friar Xil, Ribeiriña or the medieval troubadours. At first he thought that the ambiguous "amigo songs" and the emotional cross dressing they portrayed would fit the new situation. But he soon found out that there were no poetic leanings in the place. The appropriate mood was parody, the savage roasting of people, the sarcasm, the repartee. Anything for a laugh. His performances were risqué but still slightly coherent. Afterwards came the big joke. All wanted to dress up in a wild free for all. Towels and drapes were fitted according to individual taste. All the shoes in the closet clattered about and it was not surprising the long suffering neighbors complained of Juanjo having flamenco dancers at his parties.

Rosiña took cover under the table to avoid being trampled to death. The guests were already tottering and even more so with the high heels. But what is the big kick you get out of wearing these heels, trying not to fall, with painfully trounced feet?, Maruxa used to ask trying to understand their behavior.

Besides the heels, there was the fake Andalusian accent. It was customary of the audience to try to ape the speech of the Andalusian singers, their sibilant sounds, the moving of their hands at the flamboyant turnarounds, yes! Just so my pet!, and the ending up arms akimbo, holding an imaginary fringed shawl. The more the hullabaloo grew and the alcohol consumption increased, the more they felt inclined to the flamenco world. Over their deeply embedded Galician syntax, their homely phonetics, they tried to superimpose the sound of tambourines and castanets. The result was ludicrous, more so since they were unaware of it. By playacting, by overdoing life to the utmost they were able to forget their dramatic existence, appeasing their yearnings to be something different. Society alienated them, and they went on to separate even more. From this fact their social insolidarity grew. Galicia's history was alien to them; the historical circumstances of the marginality of their mother tongue, and of the people it represented, were not concern of theirs. Nationalist reivindications, working class battles, all that jazz was for others. They were outside the social pale, a cause of scorn even to those who cried solidarity, firebrands demanding a better world. These asked equality for a people of which they, the maricones, were not a part. Their rights were not their rights; justice was only for the macho world. Maricones were excluded. They were a social blight, refuse, the unmentionable. The same way Blacks were permitted to vaunt their irrationality and spontaneity by displaying their natural world of rhythm, with all the stereotypes fixed on them by their oppressors as a contrast to the reason, artifice and sophistication of the superior culture. So could these whites. Therefore, they continued to play the maricón role cast upon them, taking it to disparate extremes of affectation and mannerism. Look at us!, they seemed to broadcast, risking scorn. Look at us, parading our disgrace, spitting on our shame. They laughed about themselves. They flayed themselves in public masking their pain, reaffirming their negativity. They drowned their suffering in big bashes, parties, jokes. Lacking love kisses, they seeked in hundreds of mouths what they could rarely find in one. They needed the success of conquest, the race for pleasure. They wallowed in disproportion to match orderly society's proportion, their abnormality set against the other's normality.

Even though they had these thoughts they never talked about them. Only Juanjo discussed it with Maruxa sometimes.

"But why the insistence on Andalusian speech?" asked Maruxa indignantly. "And not only here. It happens in the whole of Spain."

"May be it's nicer to the ears," replied Juanjo just to say something.

"I don't' see that," insisted Maruxa. "Since Galego is the sweetest and softest of languages, so they say...wouldn't it be more appropriate?"

"It's not only the language. It's the movements, the dance, the tapered pants, the hip swaying, the grace...I don't know!" answered Juanjo with indifference.

"I think it's absurd," refuted Maruxa hotly. "And to tell you the truth it makes me mad. It's the same with those foreigners who believe all Spaniards are toreros and all Spanish women flamenco dancers. You are contributing to perpetuate the Spanish stereotype."

"Frankly, I can't care less about Spanish stereotypes," dismissed Juanjo airily.

"And besides," she taxed him, "you are a bunch of renegades. All of those at your parties, so sophisticated, always talking Castilian...One of these days someone is going to slip and you will get a good thrashing. I wish!" said Maruxa angrily. "I'd be delighted!"

"Don't be so hard on us, Maruxiña," said Juanjo endearingly. "Convince yourself that we are a bunch of fools. Better leave us to our foolishness. It would be too pathetic to wake up," concluded Juanjo with unusual bitterness.

"Don't change the subject. There is no excuse. And that caricature you make of women!" said Maruxa rising her voice.

"We like being feminine, like diss! What do you want?" sang Juanjo in an affected voice. "We want to be your peers, to identify with you..."

"Nonsense! You don't care about us at all! What you do is ridiculize women, making a stupid joke of us," objected Maruxa never mincing words.

Juanjo understood his friend's objections but refused to give them serious thoughts. He avoided complications. It was like riding a Ferris wheel with your eyes closed. He pursued his part tirelessly. He knew he was a role model for many, the living image of the carefree maricón, witty, bold, roguish. He was in command of the scene. He couldn't think of anything else but the playacting.

His parties lasted till dawn. The guests drank, made merry, became intimate. Couples were made and unmade. Each new party brought new love affairs.

When their legs refused to carry them further, they tried parlor games. The thing was never to let up.

"Girls!" clapped Moor-Eater. "May I have your attention. We are going for a game of blindman's buff. See who'll play the blind man. Are we all here?"

"Whispering Pines is missing," said Marysilly looking around. "Aie, look at her! How romantic, out in the balcony watching the sky!"

"Star gazer! Say, what do the stars say about our love?" asked Naparreto Jarsía holding Lammemoor's waist that came up about his nose. "Tell me it'll last an eternity."

"They say you look like the i and the dot," intervened acidly Firefly Finita while caressing Good-for-nothing Bella, a balmy blond that slept peacefully, his head on his lap.

Bella was Finita's perpetual lover and an empty headed oaf besides, but Finita had pep enough for both of them.

"Who will do the buffing?" asked Finita to Naparreto maliciously.

"Hey, you!" bristled Naparreto quite miffed. "Do you need proof? You know, small man, big dick."

"Small man, big venom, my mother used to say," replied Firefly Finita.

"She probably meant your father," said bellicose Naparreto standing on his raised toes. "I will show you what is what. You'll learn nothing from that blob you are sleeping with..."

"Let me know when you are horny!" cried Firefly Finita all ruffled up.

"But what, are you going to fight now?" slurred Juanjo with difficulty, being all soused up.

"Come on, girls, who's the blind man?" insisted Lili waving her hand. Eeny, miney, mo...It's you turn, Breaker. Sit down here."

"Let me have a bracer first. I am going to need it," he replied, flustered, while he picked a glass from a table.

They covered his eyes with a scarf. The game consisted of going by and kissing him. He had to guess who was the kisser.

"French kisses, right? No pecking," insisted Moor–Eater leading the game.

Everyone took the kissing very seriously. Perfection meant more passion, more tongue, longer time...When the kissed man guessed right, he was set free and his post taken by another. Those slow to guess had their lips chapped and full of sores the next day.

"Doooris! Where is Doris?" stammered Juanjo lying on a corner, by now totally drunk.

"They all went to Piper's, her and some others, I don't know who," replied Marysilly.

"There is no Cointreau left," stated Moor Eater shaking the bottle upside down.

"Let's go to Piper's too," proposed Juanjo trying vainly to stand up.

"We can also go to Niñé's. If you come with me, girls, drinks are free," slurred Moor Eater. "He is crazy about me!"

"It is too late now, at least five o'clock. We'll have to go to Claveles. Where is your car?" asked Flaky Olga to Moor–Eater.

"Since when do I have a car, honey? You are really flaky!"

"Plizzzz!" could hardly articulate Juanjo. "Bring me my little cape for this damp air," and he placed over his coat a short Camariñas lace cape that belonged to his grandmother Otilia.

They all met at Claveles, a roadside bar open all night. River fishermen also went there at dawn to warm their frozen bodies with aguardente before disappearing into the white mist, that milky wall encircling the river like a ghostly wraith.

In the morning, Doris managed with difficulty to get Juanjo into bed. He was so drunk that he forgot the bobby pins he put on his hair every night, covered with a thin net and a little mauve cap, matching the bed curtains. He hated his blond curls. He wanted to have straight hair, and did all he could to uncurl it. It wouldn't be the first time he showed up at the bank with a forgotten pin on his head. He couldn't understand the customers' amazement when he leaned down to pick up the money. It was a fellow worker who alerted him, and there was badinage enough for a very long time.

Other guests to his parties stayed at the Méndez Núñez. Should they have eyes and ears, those 17th century noblemen whose portraits hung on the hotel's majestic ballroom would topple in front of their extravagant behavior that weekend. Never anything like that had happened before in the history of that venerable building.

Weather permitting, the revelers would flock next day to the Guitiriz's swimming pool where they could continue shamelessly to outrage the locals.

Other times, without his father knowing, Juanjo secured his mother's permission to go to the pazo. That was a real boon. They played hide and seek in the old rooms where dark corners abounded. Many couples took their time to come out. Great passions of the night before drifted away the next morning, while other amours were born under the spell of the park, the pazo's solemn bedrooms, the aristocratic beds.

"You are a non stop lecher," said Juanjo to Naparreto who, tired of making eyes to Lucía de Lammermoor, a.k.a. Big Willow, was now angling for Firefly Finita still pissed off from the day before. Meanwhile unsuspecting Good-for-nothing Bella rested his future horns on the wool mattress of the so called Condal Suite.

Worn out by a hangover, Juanjo went for a stroll in the garden. He felt exhausted. It was not only the alcohol but the killing effort required for his performance. He was an actor on a nonstop show. Little did Merceditas know when she oriented him towards an acting career, the hard work it would entail. The world was a stage, life a play. Even though he enjoyed acting, it was tiring him out. But the show had to go on.

In one corner of the gazebo, surrounded by bushes and under a weeping willow, he found Whispering Pines.

"You do know how to pick a spot. Nothing more appropriate for your languor," ironized Juanjo with an effort.

Whispering Pines stared at him with pensive eyes.

Grateful for the silence Juanjo heaved himself down with a sigh.

"Come," said Whispering Pines setting his head on his lap. "Why don't you take a break?"

Juanjo didn't know whether he meant at that moment or he referred to the thoughts burgeoning in his head. He didn't want to enquire, afraid of being found out. He remained silent and closed his eyes while Whispering Pines massaged his temples softly. He fell asleep.

Juanjo's life moved on by fits and starts under the blowing gusts of unexpected winds.

Ignoring the warnings of caution offered by Maruxa, he defied society rules more blatantly every day. People of the hood admired his gallantry. He was famous in all Galicia, and the Lugo parties became notorious. The number of guests grew and the rowdiness at the apartment with them. Neighbors started to complain. Rumor had that he brought gypsies to the place, no doubt due to the noise of clapping heels that accompanied his songs. The gossip about the gypsies was another reason for more capers and raucous laughter giving higher intensity to the flamenco numbers.

The storm was not unleashed by the neighbors' complaints, however. The lightning hit unexpectedly one quiet morning. There was no boisterous party the day before at the apartment. A few friends had gathered to talk and had stayed overnight. Among them was Whispering Pines who, although he also lived in Lugo, had refused to go home.

Early in the morning his mother had gone to the place screaming like a madwoman My sweet little boy, she wailed, kept prisoner in that den of iniquity, that nest of maricones! My son is barely a child and those perverts have seduced him! That's statutory rape, you bloody queers! cried the lady as if possessed.

She didn't have to go far for the police. They were right there. Police officers went up the apartment and rang the bell. Half asleep, one of Juanjo's friends answered the door.

"Juanjo!" he cried. "Police!"

"Let them in, let them in! I'm waaaiting!" sang Juanjo from bed thinking it the usual joke.

They were taken to jail the way they were.

Interrogation was a vile affair. Insults from rotten mouths, threats of banishment for socially unbecoming conduct; they didn't mince words. Later the judge made them ratify their confessions not without embellishing them with more trumped charges of sexual misconduct. It reminded Juanjo of Father Puga and all the other fathers urging him to confess, confess...The judge also insisted, how? how? wanting to know, writing down details, prompting what he wanted to hear, even adding things suggested by his own sick mind. He finally sent them to prison. They created a commotion within the prison walls. Their entrance was an event. Even prison officials were nervous to receive such unusual jailbirds. Quickly the warden demanded their separation from the other inmates, so they were held incommunicado in their cells. Juanjo and his four companions wanted to believe it was all a bad dream. In a daze they were unable to understand the forces that had cast them into that hellhole. All around floated a hideous smell, a mixture of excrement, semen and human sweat made more acute by the damp walls and the outside fog drifting indoors. The yellow-gray sheets on the cell cot still showed the milky stains of the previous occupant. On the door, a set of lines made with excrement gave an account of the jackoffs the former tenant had engaged into, a sort of lonely sex boasting for lack of worthy sexual competitors.

Sunday Mass was the only chance to escape the black hole where they were buried. But Juanjo was not to be seduced by honeyed prayers. He stubbornly refused to go. Instead he secured buckets of water and a broom to clean his pigsty. 'I clean my little house, la, la, la,' he sang loudly while the others trooped to the makeshift chapel.

Once the mass began Juanjo's friends had to lean on the walls to avoid fainting. The overpowering stench of the crowd plus the church's own smell made them sick. The unfamiliar rites contributed to their discomfort. The inmates' talk drowned the prayers, their whispered jokes making fun of the celebrant...The priest went on with the Mass unfazed, ignoring the goings-on. The makeshift altar boy, a squalid lame man with a small head tried to follow the priest's orders as best he could. Now and again he tripped over the threadbare carpet, his trembling hands risking to spill the holy wine. The priest glared murderously at him often, and the poor hunchback acted even more clumsily under his silent disapproval. Each false step was a cause of mirth for the congregation. Very few followed the ritual. Most of them were on the lookout for action. Against the assumption of the prison guards, the queers did not cause trouble other than being new. If the warden knew how 'ordinary' prisoners made out among themselves, he would not have been so bent on isolating the extraordinary newcomers. The prisoner next to Whispering Pines did not waste any time, and the poor boy was horribly embarrassed. He felt many eyes on him and his cheeks were on fire. Sassy Purita was furious. They always have to go after the weakest, he thought angrily; of course, a blond chick, so delicate...and they are already at him. But one had to remain silent, lest they not be let out again.

It was not the prison officials but the other inmates, never missing a thing of what was going on outside, nobody knew how, who told them they would soon be free. Those "classy kids" never had any problems, they complained enviously. Only the pariahs remained in place. They were released on twenty-five thousand pesetas bail.

The closed room trial came out a year later. Tempers were calmer then. Even the indignant neighbors, the former complainers of the gypsy trysts, the noisy parties, declared never having witnessed anything improper. Maruxa, always the loyal friend, testified to be Juanjo's girlfriend and having an ongoing sexual relationship with him.

Juanjo's manliness was now publicly vindicated, but his disgust over the whole mess often mounted to his throat, suffocating him.

Even though he was grateful for the generosity of his character witnesses, he knew it was his clever attorney who had mainly saved the day. He alleged improper arresting procedures. According to him the police had not any business to proceed on a misconduct charge. All they could do was report the charges made by others. The trial was suspended.

Despite the success, that setback changed dramatically Juanjo's life. No parties, no friends, no more revelry. All those who had praised him so extravagently avoided him now like the plague. The habitual guests never appeared in Lugo anymore; lying low in their dens they never showed up again. It was a great blow for Juanjo. All the mess: the joint, the trial, were easy to block out. His own sense of humor could even see something jocose to be gleaned from the experience. But the ingratitude and cowardice of the hood, his closest friends with whom he had shared so many intensely happy moments...that was difficult to swallow. The rats had abandoned the sinking ship. He expected everything but that. He, Juanjo of the unfailing spirit, ready to defy anyone, even unto the whole wide world, fell into the blackest depression. He got drunk more often than ever. To cap it all, the bank ordered his transfer. Because of his family connections he would not lose his job, but he was to be sent to the faraway Monterroso branch.

He had had enough. Lugo's gray skies threatened now to crush him like a tombstone. The omnipresent mist surrounding the city, the same that had suffused his jaunty nightly countenance so poetically, pierced his body cruelly now. His zest froze up. People's misty cold eyes pricked like pins, forcing him to seek refuge or to take flight.

He remembered now Maruxa's warnings. She had been right all along. He had only to run afoul of the law to make his enemies grow in self-importance. Their power chained him forever to his own sex or better still, to his anatomy, compelling him to behave according to the norm. He was the victim of the 'normal' ones, the defenders of social order. By sacrificing him they exorcised their own ghosts; they were reassured of their macho role; they could go on with the sexual comedy, the boasting of their exemplary conduct. Juanjo could not give up his pet grievance: that unlike them, and in order to be himself, to behave the way he really was, he had to run away, leave the people he loved; give up his own country forever.

He didn't have the courage to say goodbye to his mother or his son. He left Lugo as if carried by the devil.

Chapter 4

Standing in front of the mirror, Juanjo performed his morning ritual slowly. Besides that mirror there were in the bedroom two other strategically placed so the watching game could be complete. Facing the bed, one of them reflected the quilted blue satin bedspread with valences hanging down all the way to the Persian carpet. The embroidered silk cushions placed apparently at random on top of the bed were in fact carefully arranged with art and precision. One of them showed a Moor, his copper colored chest bare, and a white turban contrasting his black locks, sitting cross–legged near a basket where a cobra was rising to the sounds of the charmer's flute. In another, the snake knotted around his neck like a living, viscose necklace. The Moor's white teeth shone between his lips while he leisurely squeezed the cobra's head close to his own mouth so that it seemed the animal's deadly kiss was about to touch him. The Moor's ascetic glass eyes betrayed no emotion.

Another mirror showed the dresser, with the shapely golden small jars engraved with oriental designs that seemed ready to store lustral water. Small carved wooden boxes laid next to an enamel jewel box with several small drawers. There were also perfume bottles in different colors.

Everything appeared in perfect symmetry, arranged as if for a theatrical performance. A deadened geometry. Objects seemed evanescent, charmed by the basilisk, frozen in time like himself, by the magic wand that enthralled Juanjo's life now. The heady atmosphere reeking of perfume contributed to the room's dreamlike appearance, to the atmosphere of ancient ritual, of bewitching spell. Mirrors multiplied and froze all images, placing people and objects on a plane of reflected irreality, like a mirage. It smelled of amber and jasmine, and a fragrance of mint escaped the steaming teacup on a small corner table. Should music be in order, it would rather be "On a Persian market" by Ketelbey.

He laid out his apparel carefully on the bedspread: underwear, dress, even the jewelry...He did it trance–like. The fear and frights of his first youth, when he used to don his mother's clothes on the sly during her absences, must have conditioned the present slow tempo of his ministrations. He hummed a casual air.

He breathed deeply the room's odors. He liked warm, deep, sweet fragrances. His mother's dresses, he remembered, had a sharp pungency of being in storage, a mixture of armpit perspiration and a soupçon of Oriental Woods mingled with camphor moth balls. When he was little he used to call the camphor 'Almanzor' making his mother laugh. How he enjoyed to see Merceditas' little dimples creasing both her cheeks. He would tiptoe to kiss her, his tongue tickling the little holes on her face till his mother would put an end to the caress with nervous laughter. At lunch time she would tell his father.

"Do you know how he calls camphor? "Almanzor'!" she laughed again. "Wasn't he a real bad Moor chief who took away the bells of Santiago's cathedral? You tell him," Merceditas encouraged her dour husband.

"Yes. And he also forced thirty virgins to go along with him," replied the father aggrandizing Almanzor's cruelties.

Later, Juanjo inquired from his mother:

"Mama, isn't Jesus' mother who is in heaven also a Virgin? Those other virgins that Almanzor took away were then her sisters?"

"They were maidens. They were called virgins at that time."

Juanjo could not understand all that fuss about virgins. Neither about the Moors, whom he confused with the wretched Saracens that the Masked Warrior of the comics used to kill all the time. Die, you infidel! he would cry blandishing his sword. In his own school encyclopedia was written that the Arabs who had conquered Spain never settled in Galicia. The city chroniclers agreed that the Arabs hadn't left any traces of their presence there. Sure, the Moor Muza had been a visitor, but he had to leave Lugo quickly when recalled to Damascus by his superiors. And he left. Soon thereafter King Alfonso I occupied the city without hindrance since Arabs and Berbers had already abandoned it. Therefore, no Arabs. However, his 'tata' María told him about the Moor caves near her village. Old women said that rich treasures the Moors had left behind still remained hidden there. Also, close to the family pazo there was a big rock people called 'Moor Rock.' One day he had climbed it while playing and he was soon warned off by an old toothless woman leading her cow to the pasture:

"Come down immediately, child! Don't climb that rock!" shouted the old woman, her sibilants escaping through the gaps of her scarce teeth.

"Why?" irritated Juanjo wanted to know.

"It's keeping the Moors in. All arrogant Moors came out through that hole till someone managed to block their path with the big rock," replied the old woman.

"Did you ever see them"? asked Juanjo.

"Not I. But my grandmother, may she rest in peace, told me that they were tall and handsome. And also rich. They had a gold chain so long that came all the way down from Fontefrida, and Castro do Outeiro till Poza Grande."

"Wow!" whistled the boy admiringly, looking up the mountain trying to figure out the chain's length.

"They must be like those Moors, so strong in their horses, that escort Franco when he goes around," mused the boy.

"Aie, they may very well be! I never saw those but maybe they also took Moors for that too," muttered the old woman pulling the cows' rope.

The Moors. All his childhood had been inspired by them. At the park a crazy woman would sing holding her skirts: "An old woman at the time of the Moors turned her ass on a bullfighter's ring, aie, lelo, lelelo, lelelo..." Everyone talked about the Moors. Even though they were never there, thought Juanjo, they surely left plenty of traces. At one time, he had been so obsessed with the Moors that he insisted on dressing up like one for the Carnival. How had he pestered one of the neighbors, a former sharpshooter in the Ifni war, to teach him how to salute in Moorish fashion!

It took him years to find out that Galician Moors had apparently nothing to do with those who had invaded the Iberian peninsula in the 8th century. Those were real; the others, the Galician ones, were pure myth.

Life was really curious, reflected Juanjo, looking at the picture of a handsome, black-eyed youth on his beside table. All that fussing about the Moors, and who would have thought I would end up living with one.

Yes, he was a Moor's lover. He had met him one night at the Ramblas.

"What a man, girlsss! Dark, shiny eyes...! What look!" explained Juanjo to the local hood. "It reaches your soul, it pierces you..."

"Don't play the romantic, will you? That Porche he owns, what, do you expect us to believe it means nothing?" his companions had replied pointedly. "Queenie, you are a real queen!" ironized one with a slap while his head rolled back and forth imitating many short and multiple car brakings.

"I cannot deny a car like that is useful. It allows you to look up others, like diss," Juanjo turned his head pretending to look a hypothetical person up and down.

He thought he would be like many others, a one night stand. But he came back. Day after day...till he got him an apartment. The Moor went crazy about him. He couldn't stand that someone else could see him, touch him...

"You are possessive like a Moor!" Juanjo flattered him pressing his head against his own small breasts which were becoming more noticeable due to the ingestion of hormones. "You are my sultan and I am your odalisque," and other similar silly endearments and nonsense.

"No! You are my walkyria!" corrected the Moor, hungry for Juanjo's blond, Nordic beauty.

With one thing and another he had been with him for two years now.

He stared at the outfit on top of the bed. Everything was in exquisite taste. Mohammed wanted nothing but the best for him.

He dressed as a woman only occasionally, when they were going out. Mohammed traveled a lot; his job, he said. Sometimes he was away for weeks. And they did not go out often. He came home tired, and all his energies were reserved to enjoy his "walkyria." Otherwise Juanjo dressed informally: blue–jeans and wide sweaters to hide the effect of hormones on his breasts, his hair pinned in a pony tail. He hardly went out. He shopped at the local market but for that purpose it was better to dress as a man. He didn't have to wait in line and the sellers treated him royally. "Just a moment, if you don't mind, madam. Let me take care of the gentleman quickly..." Those courtesies made Juanjo feel like a Valladares again. He tried to have a full refrigerator at all times. If Mohammed preferred to stay cooped up at home for several days, he wanted to have plenty of food available. He liked his cooking, which felt exotic to his African palate. Certainly, Juanjo was a good cook. He imitated grandmother Otilia's quick, precise strokes when preparing an empanada with the fresh eels just bought. Juanjo seemed to hear the dry thuds against the marble surface, dough stretched out like a tongue, kneaded again with suet to give it a flaky consistence. Sitting on a stool in a corner of the kitchen, Juanjo used to admire her adroitness, breaking up the pinions fallen from the pine cones used to heat the stove and roasting them on the fire.

When Mohammed, the Moor, was away, Juanjo went to his English class in the afternoon. Sometimes he made a quick getaway to have coffee with old friends. He didn't want to be away from home too long. He lived a cloistered life. If the Moor called up and he was not there...Saint Xil!

Because of his staying home so much, Juanjo became friendly with Sabela, a girl from Xinzo who lived next door. She worked as a hostess at an American bar. In order to justify her working hours she told the other tenants she was a night nurse.

"In fact that's what you are," mused Juanjo who had grown to despise all sex beggars.

Sabela avoided to give the neighbors food for rumor. She wanted to come and go unnoticed.

"Gee, baby, with that air of Theresian nun you have, I'm not surprised they do not suspect you...," teased Juanjo when he ran into her at the market mousy-looking in a pleated skirt and a tucked white blouse.

They never suspected him, that is to say her, either. When in drag he tried to leave home surreptitiously to avoid recognition. However, he was not recognized even when they did see him. The first floor neighbor, one of the nosy Parkers of the area, used to throw him a line now and then.

"What chicks visit you, young man! The one I saw yesterday leaving your place was a knockout..." drooled the old man over his now scant mustache.

"Pay no attention to him," cut in his wife sarcastically. "He is jealous," she changed her tone. "But she was so beautiful and elegant though..."

"She was a friend of Mohamed's," lied Juanjo.

"Well, see that you get one like that for yourself," advised the old man ironically.

At times like that he wanted to blurt out: It's me. That's how beautiful I am. It took a big effort to keep silent, but he didn't want any trouble. Who would have thought it! He who had been so fond of boasting, and now acting so meek, keeping up appearances. Before he used to be bold, but now he held his peace. He had lost much of his former arrogance, he didn't know how. Money problems were possibly at the root of his transformation. Power and might grew along with riches. He who has the bucks, has the power; those who pay have rights. Poverty had dampened his pride. He had even worked as a male prostitute, internalizing the masochism necessary for the job. Therefore he bit his tongue to avoid telling the impertinent neighbor the truth: that he himself was the knockout. He had no other option but silence, although his double life provided him still with a morbid complacence. In the building, the neighbors called him "the maricón on the third floor," but they were civil and greeted him cordially albeit with a certain astonishment.

Now he didn't believe the word "maricón" offensive. In times past he had resorted to fistfights in more than one occasion because of that word. Not anymore. It was a mark of pride, gay pride, thought Juanjo laughing at himself. He remembered one discussion with a gay activist that his friend K, the man of the valise, had introduced to him. It was in the first weeks of his arrival in Barcelona. He could listen to him now. "We have to reject the term homosexual," said the activist. "It is too technical. It is convenient for experts or doctors, but the right term to use is maricón. It rings a proper bell. It is forceful. We have to accept it as our trademark," he stated emphatically, playing on his scanty beard with his slender fingers.

"Don't you see it as an insult?" protested Juanjo. "It is pejorative."

"More to the point. If we adopt it, it will stop. It will become normal. They call us maricones? All right, maricones we will be! That's where our struggle must begin," concluded the other firmly on a preaching tone.

"Accepting their scorn, right?" rejected Juanjo.

"No," replied the other, "hitting them on the face with it. Look at the blacks, for instance. The poorest, the more wretched are ashamed of being black, and try to whiten their skin, even stretch their kinky hair. Anything to disguise their blackness. They also consent to be called euphemisms, like African Americans, people of color...Rubbish! Niggers! The first step for them is to want to be a nigger, being proud of the name just as they think it an insult now."

"Yes, maybe," mused Juanjo. "Being a nigger is even worse than being a maricón."

"Unless you are a maricón and a nigger," retorted the gay activist laughing at his own wit.

"You said that the first step was to accept ourselves as social niggers. And then?" asked his friend K, who, nevertheless the diffidence of his puny figure, always pursued an argument till the end.

"Then? That's clear," and the activist paused scratching his scruffy beard as if the red stubble would drop pearls of wisdom. "Instead of wishing to become white, the opposite. We'll make the whites niggers, give them nigger features or nigger culture...Brief, making them want to be us."

"You mean for us the second step would be to make everyone a maricón...That's a laugh, dude!" cried K, amused.

"But they are already!," Juanjo jumped on his favorite subject. "They do not come out of the closet because they are afraid, otherwise you'd see..."

"Hold it, hold it," said the activist taking his hand away from his goatee to make him stop. "Let's not oversimplify. There are many who repress it, I agree, but to say that all..."

"Were it not for their repressive upbringing, the social stigma, public opinion...You'd see!" insisted Juanjo. "Otherwise, why that visceral rejection? You explain it to me. Give me a good reason!"

"They despise what they don't know. They can't stand difference," orated his opponent in a solemn tone but without much conviction. He paused and then changed his tune. "Dude, you demolish all arguments with your glib tongue!"

"Never better said," said K ironically, showing his perfect teeth in a wide grin.

"We are fighting for the recognition of our difference," insisted the activist, "and now you come and tell us that the others are not different..." He moved his head while his fingers tangled with his beard again: "You are going too far—at least for now. We will see in the long run...but for the time being we must defend our dignity as different people," he concluded the speech sure of himself.

This and other opinions reaffirmed Juanjo in his condition during his first weeks in Barcelona. It was also a matter of pride to know that many artists, writers, theatrical people...understood. So-and-so! and they would name a successful artist of the moment, he is even more maricón that I! He heard it all the time in artistic circles. His own father, thought Juanjo, must have known or guessed it, even then, when he decried to Merceditas his son's dedication to the performing arts.

Juanjo had the opportunity to find out many things at the time of his friendship with K, the man of the valise. They had become friendly soon after Juanjo's arrival in the city. He was a thin, unprepossessing young man in floating long white shirts, too big for his meager body, over his narrow black pants. His too long shoes ended in pointed curlicues giving them the appearance of Moorish slippers. The oriental air of his footwear was at odds with the black valise he always carried with him. He looked like a figure on a Kandinsky painting. Black mascara thickened his eyelashes over two eyes quiet as peaceful lakes. He exuded tenderness. His personality, only his personality, reminded Juanjo of Whispering Pines. At that time they used to visit art exhibitions where he introduced Juanjo to the world of line and color. On Sundays they also went to concerts. He was able to meet some of the country's intelligentsia but he never became an initiate. Most of all Juanjo met with Galician immigrants, or their sons, who abounded in the city. However, in the places where homosexuals gathered, there were people from all over Spain. Although most of them were from Andalucía, it really didn't matter where they came from. In that gathering of fallen angels, solidarity was their only country.

To his friend of the valise he called K not because of Kandinsky, for at that time he didn't know the painter or his works, but for Kafka. He was happening to read *The Metamorphose* at the time they met. His friend changed shapes with such grace and creativity that Juanjo teased him: yours is a real Kafkaesque metamorphose even though you have nothing to do with choleoptera...So the name K stuck.

It took him a long time to know what the mysterious valise contained. Quite simply it was a pair of shoes and a normal outfit to wear when returning home. He lived with his family and worked mornings as a draftsman. He couldn't afford to play the innocent game of drag metamorphose openly.

K opened a new world for him, pointing out a new road where he would have liked to walk, but all that was finished now. That road had closed like so many other roads in his life. Like Maruxa, K had been a great listener to his confidences. Juanjo was still a talker, garrulous and simpático, but very few people knew him or his true feelings intimately. First his mother, then Maruxa, K...The rest was idle talk.

He and K walked the lower city barrios with their atmosphere of Jewish craftsmen quarters, the old medieval guild alleys pierced by the sun. The clean, powerful sun was very different from the veiled, shy rays that bathed his country in the very few sunny days of grayish Lugo. They lingered on the benches of the small plazas that had kept their provincial charm, their flavor of fruit and the market place. There they talked and talked.

"To what do you attribute the fact," asked Juanjo going back to the topic, "that so many artists get along so well with us?"

"They say that we, homosexuals, are more sensitive..." K's voice was laden with irony. Then he went on more seriously: "I don't know much about it but it would be interesting to research into the subject, starting with the true practitioners of the gay-learning, the gay-science...For there are so many. And not only artists but thinkers, scientists, and even warriors...Remember Plato, Alexander, Erasmus, Shakespeare, Leonardo da Vinci, Julio César, Benavente..." recited K.

"Don't go on. And what if we added those who understand and don't know or don't want to know...?" insinuated Juanjo.

"I know what you mean," interrupted K. "You'll come to affirm that all great men were homosexuals," and he looked reproachfully at Juanjo who laughed maliciously, like a mischievous child. "But, look," reasoned K smugly, "the argument can be turned around. We can make a list of homosexual geniuses, true. But who can count the ones who were not or are not? Don't you understand?" insisted K. "Always the same song: trying to lean on something. Always justifying ourselves."

"May be so," agreed Juanjo. "But it also helps to debunk myths, as an antidote to prejudice. For example: do you like Tchaikovsky's music, Whitman's poetry or Tennessee Williams' plays? They were geniuses, right? Well, deal with it, they were maricones!" concluded Juanjo triumphantly as if he had crushed a hypothetical opponent in front of him.

"And you so happy with your childish revenge!" commiserated K. "You can't understand that that argument is inappropriate, even detrimental to our interests. That line of reasoning leads to the conclusion there is something physical, some special cells, a different essence in us homosexuals. It's the capstone to biological argument. We reject biological principles to single out our difference. Otherwise we would carry the notion that ours is a disease, a physical disturbance that makes us neurotics or psychos..."

"Who says that?" replied Juanjo. "It isn't necessary to allege biological traits. To my knowledge *they* do not resort to biology to justify the existence of artists, thinkers, avant-garders or revolutionaries among them. Who said they were provided with exquisite, outstanding neurones? Who said it is the cells that store sensitivity or artistic faculties? Not at all. It is more the sociological or psychological forces at work, don't you see? In our specific case, I believe it is not farfetched to argue that the same marginality that society imposes upon us is not too negligible a cause of our artistic tendencies. It has been suffered in solitude, and creativity is a way out. If we were happy and satisfied, we would not be creative. We would be contented just to live and enjoy life," concluded Juanjo.

"Your argument rests on a romantic notion of artistic creativity. They want us to believe an artist is a highly suffering, lonely, pale human being..." satirized K. "Do you know?" and he couldn't suppress a laugh that, like white lightning, illuminated his face, "when I was a teenager I had read, don't know where, that many artists, outstanding individuals and even saints had suffered from TB. Since I wanted to be an artist, I used to drink vinegar secretly to become pale and emaciated, an artist at last!" he laughed at his own foolishness. "If I knew then the theory of homosexual savants I would have come straight out of the closet instead of fighting myself so hard."

"You see how useful it is?" Juanjo ran to the breach opened by K. "You are a skeptical man. But no matter how much you deny it, you must agree that artists are people out of the mainstream. That's why they create alternate worlds, human beings, beauty..."

"I know many malcontents, wretched or marginated people who never wrote a poem or even read it," demurred K sarcastically.

"Because they are illiterate among other things. Bah! It is useless to argue with you," said Juanjo considering the matter closed.

He remembered his conversations with K while putting on the finishing touches. How far they were now! He admired with pleasure the changes taking place in his body while he let a pearl rope slide between his small breasts, like a nubile odalisque. This way we arrive at the biological, he heard's K's voice like an echo. He had arrived at the biological another way. He lovingly encased his small breasts into a black lace bra, turning this way and that to admire them in profile, thrusting his chest straight forward. He caressed them, lifting them up in his hand towards the mirror, as an offering. The gesture reminded him of Our Lady of the Big Eyes who also held her breast in her hand to entice the hungry baby she held in her arms. Her absent eyes, however, made her look more like a nanny; they did not portend she would ever nurse a child. He couldn't either. His boobs were not a mother's; they were ornamental. He forgot the Virgin and lowered his lids as a vamp would. He had changed a lot over the years. He didn't know how, but after playing the woman for so long he was quickly becoming one. Of the hardiness of the first times, when he desired men as his equals, when the other's virility matched his, so different from feminine softness, very little remained. He was getting mellow. The first times out of the closet he manifested proudly his sexual preference. Maruxa, his great friend Maruxa, couldn't understand it. He could still listen to her:

"Really, pal, yours...well, I respect, but I can't understand. How can you dislike us women, who are prettier, softer, sweeter...Buddy, when you can have a beautiful girl in your arms...how can you prefer another beard, more hair, another...?"

"Yes," avowed Juanjo frankly. "We prefer the ruggedness of our equals. There is no higher pride than seducing your own likeness," and he repeated the spontaneous phrase without thinking, finding it to his taste. "Forces are measured up between equals."

"You are talking in terms of a struggle. Men are always the same, dealing with war and violence, even for..."

"And what is love but a struggle?" interrupted Juanjo.

"Love," scorned Maruxa. "What love are you talking about? You won't call love that messing and drooling about seeking an orgasm..."

"Saint Maria Goretti!" teased Juanjo kneeling in front of her, his hands joined in prayer.

To maintain pride, dignity and even virility one needed money, position, power. When he arrived at Barcelona he had tried to fend for himself. He did everything. He sold books, made surveys...He walked the city from one end to another, letting himself be carried by her. His greatest delight was to find the sea unexpectedly in his walks. A sea that was heralded by the smell of tar, of salt, and finally showing up dazzlingly, in sun-faded blue. After so much walking under that burning glare, he missed sometimes the Lucense fog, the coolness of the damp cobbles instead of these sun scorched buildings. He dreamed of oak coppices while contemplating the Modernist homes of the city, full of bourgeois self-importance as proof of the mercantile wealth of the inhabitants. The opulence he saw, or thought he saw, intensified his own misery. Those jobs helped him get to know the city, but nothing else. He couldn't find his own niche. He even suffered hunger. He had to fight off the temptation of going back to Lugo. He got drunk often.

He didn't have any choice but to go into one of the red light district bars to serve drinks. The owner, an indecent pimp, exploited him mercilessly. But that was the only way out. He soon dominated the place.

His black lace garters and matching bra, framed his round testicles and the pink, fleshy penis emerging between the curly blond hair. He had to dye it blond to please his Moor who was crazy about golden hair everywhere, even there. He loved his blue eyes reflecting the blackness of his own; his dick, so well-endowed and fair in contrast with the Moor's bluish member; his soft, hairless body under the dark carpet of his Moorish chest.

He thought he dominated the place but it was the other way. Of course he became known, not as the Widow Roquefort but as the "Dandy." The name had been given him for his straight figure, the way he carried himself erect, just like his father, the good manners taught by his mother, his personal grooming habits, his shoes always shiny...nothing, really. But among the others, the habitual clientele, he stuck out. What would his mother say if she saw him there? Saint Xil! A Valladares among that riffraff! The worse of everything: thieves, knife-wielding mobsters...all jumbled together in small joints where they could hardly move, knocking glasses and asses around. One could find everything in those hellholes, but most of all "mariquitas," queers showing off the feather, hip-swaying their lives away in scorn, in histrionic laughter, cheapening their gracesss, aie!!!. They exaggerated their movements, fluttering their big hands like vultures over their prey, even though they were victims, exhausted, cracking themselves open to the night, to the hazards, drinking to oblivion. The feminine parody, the imitation of the stereotype, the defiant transvestism...All that "queer" acting evinced, even within the hood, sympathy on some, a disdainful smile in others and even indignation among those offended by such carryings on, such vulgar behavior. Among the last ones there were those who defended the dignity of homosexuality, gay pride, the virility of their difference which they refused to identify with those buggers. The reject of the false feminine lied at the far end of this male disapproval, as in the case of Azucena.

Azucena was a mousy wisp, a good girl looking like a country señorita, a provincial, as Merceditas would put it. She made a wry face to all those plumed fantasies. Very seldom did she appear at the hood. The maricones' brazen behavior disgusted her. She saw their blatant actions as an attack on the genuine femininity she represented. With pointed, modest reserve, she turned her head not to witness their abuse or listen to their queer profanity. "Aiiii!" the mariquitas would cry. "Be careful! You'll scare Miss Porcelain!" They ridiculed Azucena's restraint when, pursing her lips and pushing away some strands escaping her orderly hairdo, she would comment: "How silly you are!" Her voice betrayed a scrupulous accent, a delicacy of manner. Were it not for her voice, Azucena would embody femininity itself. She still had her male genitals, but she was a woman at heart. She always dressed like a girl, even to go to work. Her female attire was not a disguise, the nightly mask of some. Nor was it the creative game of K. Her outfit was never funny, loud, provoking or imaginative. She wore a wide skirt, a blouse and a wool cardigan. The way it became a nice girl, well-behaved and looking for a serious boyfriend to make her forget the existence of all other men. Azucena fitted better among the country girls, arm-in-arm with her workmates to protect themselves from the attacks of brutal country bumpkins. "Always looking for a pass, honey, are they coarse!" She liked to talk about the wedding of one of her friends: "How wonderful, the happiest day of your life, I'm sure." Other times she visited another who just had a baby girl: "She's so cute! Just like her father!" That was Azucena's lot, not the Barrio Chino where she hardly showed up at all. Juanjo became her champion when the mariquitas' deadly wit preyed too much on her. She didn't belong. She never scored. How could she in such a place! Azucena would never go to bed except in a serious relationship.

This way we arrive at the biological. The phrase kept preying on his mind. He gathered his testicles carefully with his hand, and stretched his penis, now in soft repose. Was this a man? Just because he had that thing, was he a man? He looked at his budding boobs, erect under the black lace bra. His breasts made him a woman, down below he was a man. What was he? Which bulge, which prominence held his true identity? Juanjo mused: were those pieces of flesh, those muscles, more important than feelings, urges, desires...? He could pass for a man; he could also pass for a woman. But, who asked him what he wanted to be? No one. There was no free choice in sex. When they were kids they used to be asked what they wanted to be as adults. One could answer: doctor, fireman, trapeze artist...but....Juanjo imagined Merceditas' friends' faces should he have replied: a woman. Shocking! It was impossible. When he was born, they allotted him an identity, and he could not get out of it. It was pre-determined and self-determining. When leaving his mother's womb, the midwife and the doctor had said: a boy!, and that was it. The experts in anatomy had decided for him.

He felt his penis harden a little under the pressure of his fingers. And what if he refused to be in one piece but just so, a little man and a little woman...? Azucena wouldn't. She had a beacon guiding her. She was not mixed up. She knew where her true identity lied. She was determined to suppress her male genitals, the only manly thing she owned, which, in her opinion, were useless to her. On the contrary, her packet bothered her. She felt uncomfortable with that thing hanging between her legs. She wanted to have only one sex, true, as the gods ordered. Her penis was an error, a mistake of nature. Azucena was saving up money to have an operation and be rid of that thing, thought Juanjo while his hand encircled his own beloved, hard glistening penis. He cannot, indeed he never could resist the excitement when looking at himself in the mirror, when touching himself. The sexual fantasies that others used to bestow on an object, Juanjo reverted to himself. Whenever he masturbates, he never thinks of anybody. His own image is enough to feel his penis grow and the pleasure going up his body. When he is in a passion about himself, everybody disappears: Christians or Moors.

The sunrays were coming down now. Night heralds its arrival, although it is not there yet. The diffuse light of the street lamps would soon filter through the window, enveloping the room on a cold, ghostly hue. For his musings, Juanjo loved that cool atmosphere, that throbbing shadow. He wouldn't turn the lights on unless it was necessary. Lying on his bed, he let himself go, waiting to see cars and pedestrians projected on the bedroom ceiling like imaginary travelers going through the walls in a somber parade. They were like the "santa compaña," a procession of ghosts, without lights to guide them, country lanes to scour or mist to hide within. Just black shadows. Juanjo held on to them as a lifesaver, in order not to turn completely into nothingness. In this hypnotic trance, he would sometimes fall asleep.

Now he hastened to turn the light on and finish getting ready. He would be there soon. His lover, by the way, also questioned his sex. He seemed to hear him. You are only half woman! the Moor would tell him to his face, in an outburst of scorn. What! Juanjo would remonstrate, what is missing then? I have what you like, right? Do you want any more holes to stick it in? he finished his attack in sarcasm.

His life with him, the hefty Moor, soon became a living hell. Gone was the former politeness, his Oriental courtesy, Juanjo told his friends, when he would even open the car door ceremoniously for him—big queen, big queen! cried the mariquitas with glee. Or his delicacy in giving him presents with a princely gesture...Of all that, nothing remained. Before, he never returned from a trip without a gift. A jewel, perfume, a scarf...And then, such gorgeous clothes—oh, my Moorish king!—the Arab garb he wore at home. Juanjo was dying to have one—please give me a candora!—but the Moor refused. It would never do with his blond, exotic, walkyria-like beauty that he admired so much.

Where had all that lover's devotion gone? At first, when he was away, Juanjo thought he was late on purpose. Juanjo felt, anticipated his car, his claxon, his way of parking. Juanjo would count the hours his lover was absent. He still did now, but for different reasons. How can anybody change so much? He didn't seem the same person. He seemed to find pleasure in insulting, heaping scorn upon him, with those metallic words he uttered over his lover's body. Juanjo avoided to look into his eyes when he talked like that. They were malignant, shining like those of a wounded wolf. They reminded him of the stories that María used to tell him in the village. Year after year, winter after winter, someone going through the mountains had felt the wolf's presence and his hair would stand on end, like a punkie, who also looked like they have seen a wolf. He would return home trembling, and it would take him days to speak and recover his normal countenance,. Juanjo also escaped the Moor's eyes, and for a moment he thought he heard wolf howls coming out of his Moorish mouth, a half open mouth showing his teeth, sharp and ready. But it wasn't like that. Juanjo realized later that it was nothing of the kind. The Moor's eyes were not an animal's. They were two pieces of mineral: hard and jet black, and unbreakable as rhinestone.

Feeling utterly miserable, broken down by disappointment, Juanjo could not get over it. You are a masochist, a masochist, he would repeat, but he could not stop loving him, feeling like a crumbling sand castle every time he looked at him with desire. With him Juanjo had felt desired like never before. The Moor had a natural tenderness, an ease in his movements and his manners which did not seem contrived. They were not courtesy norms just to show in public. In private he was the same way. He opened doors for him with the same charm he opened his legs. He entered him in a whirlwind of pleasure. Without giving him time to react, he lorded over him, body and soul. He was a natural in his charm and strength. He was all powerful. My king!

The Moor passed from verbal insults to blows. The same silky, lovemaking hands he used to impart pleasure all over his body, were used now to beat him up. How could he put up with it? He, who was always so bold...This Saracen gave me a potion of those they use in his country, and has me hooked on drugs. Juanjo tried to make excuses. Potion my foot, what happened is that you lost your pride, a small internal voice would refute. His parents' image would come to mind, and he couldn't block it away even rubbing his eyes purposely. His father, leaning on a cane so as not to fall, avoided to look at him. He covered his face with his hand, ashamed, a study in sadness. His mother would melt into tears, but she did look at him, and Juanjo could still feel her love. He would cry out as possessed when this happened. But what could he do? Where would he go? To the street again, in fear? Begging from door to door? Here he had a home of sorts, a life...He didn't lack anything.

He felt the satin dress slide down his body in a cold caress that made his hair prickle. He breathed deeply its shady perfume. All of a sudden, another acrid smell came to him, so strong that he seemed to breathe it anew. It was his mother's, the one that gave him the greatest excitement, the greatest pleasure. The dress clung to his body, offset his limbs. How he delighted on him! Nothing could match the joy of looking at himself. Even when he was a kid, he loved his own reflection. Afterwards, during the clandestine crossdressings in his mother's bedroom, he had enjoyed his own body, his own sexual favors, in love with his own flesh that, under the appearance of his body, would become for a moment his mother's. At that time, he did it shyly, as if committing a sin. But not anymore. The bad conscience, even any kind of conscience had soon disappeared. No one like me! he said aloud raising his arms to arrange his locks over his shoulders. His blond curls came down framing his face. The hair is everything, his mother used to say. The things he had done to straighten it...the roll, the tight net overnight...Not so now. Now he let his hair fly loose and free, in a word, he was without constraint.

Sabela, the neighbor, had set the rollers and combed his mane. She was very good at it.

"Why don't you become a hairdresser? You have such a knack! My head looks preciousss," exclaimed Juanjo while Sabela fixed his hair.

"Why, silly, I do other heads...hairless ones," laughed Sabela maliciously, pursing her fleshy mouth's, thick, prominent lips. "They are a lot more profitable. And you should see how they curl, without any rollers!"

Sabela wouldn't risk a part-time job. She needed money every month. She had her daughter at a nun's boarding school, one of the best. Pictures of her baby, María, who looked exactly like her mother, were scattered around the house. One of the topics of conversation between Juanjo and Sabela were their respective children. They even made projects to marry María to Xil René, as if they were old hidalgos deciding on an advantageous family match.

"While I live and breathe, she won't lack a thing," swore Sabela. "When I have to deal with a stinking customer with noxious breath—there are some whose mouth is like a sewer sticking down onto my body like a poultice—I need to think of my little girl to bear it. How I wish I could tell them to go to hell, to give their bad breath to their whoring mothers..."

"It's not their poor mothers' fault," objected Juanjo.

"Bah, you know what I mean," said Sabela patting his arm playfully. "You don't know what I have to put up with...The worst of every family..."

"Oh, I know some..." answered Juanjo with a knowing air.

"But for her, for my baby, I'll do anything," insisted Sabela with another conspiratorial pat on his arm.

"Why don't you bring her over here?" asked Juanjo. "She needs her mother's love...

"What are you saying!" she snapped outraged, hitting his arm with more force. "My baby in this filth! Give me a break!" she hit him again. "What could I tell her when she asked me where I went at night? No way! She will be a true señorita. She'll never know the truth."

"I don't know what is best for her. At school, without the love of her family...At least you could leave her with your parents in the village. She would be better off there..."

"What?" Sabela's eyes drew bolts of lightning while she hit his arm with renewed strength. "You don't know what you're saying. God willing, my daughter would never set foot there; not in my parent's house, nor in the village. And me neither. I left the place with my big belly, crying my eyes out...I went through hell, but I'll never go back. Never!"

"What about your daughter's father?" ventured Juanjo softly, not to rile her up. He was tired of all the hitting; the worst thing about Sabela when she got angry.

"My daughter doesn't have a father," said Sabela considering the matter closed.

Juanjo could not understand Sabela's attitude. He knew there were plenty young women like her who had illegitimate children. There were many in all Galician villages, but nobldy felt any revulsion. It was some time till he found out what Sabela had not told anyone. One Sunday, when they shared confidences while drinking gin, he learned that Sabela had been raped by her own father.

"Creeps! That is to say that María is both your daughter and your sister at the same time...What a family tangle," he joked lamely to hide his confusion.

He had thought that nothing could faze him, that no human behavior could shock him, but he was wrong. He knew those things happened, but to find it live under his eyes, to see Sabela opening her wound of shame in front of him—left him confused. He hugged her for a while, the time necessary to hide his distress.

"What did your mother do?" he inquired a little later.

"She cried with me. She cursed him freely...but she didn't dare to face him. You know him well, my sweet Sabeliña, she said, you know he is capable of killing me or kicking me out. And where would I go? I have all these little ones to care for, she said referring to my younger brothers. Pepiño, Sabina's son, seems to me he cares for you. Why don't you marry him? she suggested as a remedy."

"So, you had a boyfriend?" asked Juanjo.

"I was dating Pepiño, a nice boy. According to him, he was madly in love with me, but as soon as he found out, he left in a hurry, not without throwing to my face that I had given my father what I had refused him...So I gathered my things, which were a precious few, and left. First I went into service, at the place of a rich fishery owner in Vigo. Then...well, here I am."

Juanjo lined his eyelashes with green pencil. He had read in a magazine that green favors blue eyes. His lipstick matched the fuchsia pink of his dress, the fucking pink, he spelled out while pushing the tip of his tongue between his teeth in a captivating "move." He then laughed, displaying his perfect teeth. Captivating! The word reminded of his own captivity, prisoner of the Moor without any Masked Warrior to save him. Nowadays masks were for fun or fraud, never a true warrior's disguise. Make love, not war, said the slogan. Equally macabre.

Make yourself pretty, the Moor had told him on the phone. We are going out to dinner with friends, and I want you to make a good impression. How silly. As if he needed any recommendation. He applied pink shadow to his eyelids. Harmony was the key to elegance. Now perfume; he had to think which one would go best...The coral necklace; no, it killed the color of his dress. Better seek contrast; that shade didn't really go with any gemstone. He decided on a thick golden rope form where a small life key hung. An Egyptian touch, simple and exotic at the same time. He looked at the mirror one last time. He was all woman. No one, seeing him, would doubt it. Should you be a real woman you wouldn't worry so much about it, Sabela had told him once. His was a mirage. What does a woman feel when she makes herself pretty, when she looks at herself in the mirror. What does a woman feel when she lies with a man, when he touches her, when he crushes her, when he enters her, when...There were moments when he wanted to feel like a woman. He looked like a woman, but he knew he could not have their body experiences. What if he really had a woman's body? Then perhaps he could be all woman, like his mother, as beautiful as his mother...

He was on the lookout for the Porsche. He knew his claxon. He distinguished it from all cars. Before, he spent hours in anxiety, waiting, and when he heard it, he rushed madly down the stairs, after checking there were no open doors in the hallways. Even if they didn't recognize him, even if they did not relate him to the maricón on the third floor, one had to be cautious, and show oneself the least possible. He would fly then, despite the high heels. They gave him no trouble anymore. He wore soft, custom made leather shoes. The heels were not too high either. His Moor had told him, when he still told him these things, that he didn't want to raise his head too much when he wanted to look at those beautiful blue sapphires he had on his face...

From those endearments he went on to bad words and mistreatment. Things were not going well for him. He had business difficulties, he avowed. Sometimes he stayed at home in a foul mood. Juanjo could not understand that. If he had problems, why was he at home, instead of being out solving them?

At first, he tried to overlook his outbursts. Perhaps a bad turn, caused by his problems...But things escalated. So much that Juanjo began to rebel. What? He was also a man, a Valladares! What did that fucking Saracene think? If I were you, I wouldn't put up with it, said Sabela, encouraging him.

Arguments and screams began to increase. While the Moor was out,

Juanjo had time enough to think and increase his hatred. You can't go on like that, said Sabela, the neighbors are beginning to object, and the janitress told me it would not be tolerated much longer, that this was a respectable house. They were right, thought Juanjo, I have to end this. I have a good kitty, and soon I will tell the Moor to go fuck himself...Juanjo could not suppress a grin at his own wit. A car horn cut his reverie short.

The day was coming to a close. From the street corner, disheveled, trying to control her agitation, Sabela, the girl from Ginzo, saw Juanjo arrive. She threw herself at him almost breathless, as if she had been running.

"Finally! she cried. "Where have you been?"

"What is the matter," asked Juanjo. "You look frightened...What happened to you?"

"To me? To you something is going to happen! Your...the Moor is there...dead!" she said pointing at the house. "Full of blood...stabbed, lying on the bed...mutilated...Ugh! Butchery!"

"What?" "Are you...? But, what are you saying?" stammered Juanjo.

"It wasn't you, right? You would never..." she grabbed Juanjo's arm and shook him.

"What? Are you crazy?" answered Juanjo also holding onto her.

People were staring at them. Sabela noticed it and pulled Juanjo by the arm. They walked away from the house.

"Shh! Be quiet!" ordered Sabela. Sweatdrops fell from her brow, even though the afternoon had grown cooler.

"Enough tomfoolery!" cried Juanjo. "I don't know what you are talking about so mysteriously. Tell me clearly!"

"Couldn't be more clear. Your...your Moor has been stabbed. Brutally. If you had seen it. Some sight. The whole room full of blood."

"But who? By whom?"

"You, of course," answered Sabela with conviction. "They think you did it. The janitress, the neighbors...they are all telling the police about your arguments, the shouting, the beatings...The one on the second floor said that she heard you threatening him. One of these days I will finish you off, I swear! it seems you screamed at him."

"Saint Xil! But why? Why?" Bewildered, Juanjo couldn't stop asking.

"You even have to ask? They say it was a crime of passion. According to the police, the m.o., the atmosphere, the blood, all is normal in such crimes. The first floor busybody assures that you were jealous of a gorgeous woman who used to go out with the Moor at times. Oh, jealousy! It is so powerful! repeats the dirty old man full of righteousness. He seemed to be so nice, so soft spoken...we never know what we are capable of in such moments, when we are crazy..."

"Saint Xil! And now? I didn't do it, Sabeliña, you know I didn't—" he almost lifts her up, crushing her, trying to convince her.

"Who were you with today?" inquired Sabela.

"No one. I was walking alone. The day was so beautiful, the first nice day of the spring. I needed to go out, walk around, feel free. He, the Moor, left yesterday and I didn't expect him back for a week at least. I went out to breathe, and also to think...to think how to get out of this filth...Sabela..."—and Juanjo could not suppress his tears.

"Please, don't go on. Now is not the time to get sentimental. I hope you are not crying for him, that louse, may God forgive me!," spat Sabela crossing herself.

"I'm not crying for him, but for me. For me that..." sobs Juanjo. "The whole day I had a bad feeling. I felt a bad omen."

"So you were alone...Nobody saw you? You didn't talk to anyone?"

"No. I just wandered around the streets. I went up to the Tibidabo. I hadn't been there since the first times in Barcelona. I wanted to be alone, I tell you. I was totally upset..."

"Well, you are in a good pickle," Sabela shook her head.

"They can't blame me. I didn't do it!" repeated Juanjo.

"How can you prove it? Tell me!" remonstrated Sabela." If you show your face there, you'll go to the slammer."

The slammer again, thought Juanjo, but now the matter was more serious...

"And my things, Sabela? I have everything in that house," said Juanjo.

"They wouldn't be of any use to you, unless you want to make yourself pretty for the prison warden," said Sabela with pitiless irony.

"You are cruel. It's my whole life there..."

"Your life is precisely what you have to save now," cut Sabela. "I brought your checkbook from my house, the one you gave me for safekeeping. Do as I say. Take a powder."

Chapter 5

That was the way the woman had to push dogs away from her path. Like a queen, she walked hard as granite, her cheekbones arrogant, high and defiant like her breasts; her blue eyes giving off provoking sparks. The proud carriage was softened by the sensual and fleshy lips, opened in a dazzling smile. That's the way she appeared, and no one was immune to her charms. On the street and elsewhere. As soon as she entered a bar, a coffee shop, everyone's eyes were pinned on her. From the barstools, from the tables, alone or with company, all admired her tall figure and felt attracted to the proud femininity she displayed, the abundance of her attributes. What a woman! Thus Juanjo went on, knowing himself, herself, admired. She coquettishly increased the swaying of the hips while walking. If the eye contact persisted, Juanjo, always direct in his gaze before, had by now learned to give in. His eyelids half closed in a foxy and shortsighted glance, feigning false modesty or the appearance of being chastened. He had found out that men do not tolerate women challenges for long. Even if at first they want a hint of war in a defiant look, pretty soon they need to feel the willing surrender in order to walk tall in conquered terrain. Juanjo gave in like the woman he was, or wanted to be. He was playing with a compass in search of the female dawn.

He still enjoyed silks, soft fabrics that stuck to his body, outlining his forms like a second skin. He never wore any underwear, not even panties. Knowing Juanjo it could be said that it was to make his body conspicuous so that the Xray eyes fastened on him could make out the woman without any impediment, leaving nothing to imagination. Yes. But also, or above all, it was to feel himself and his new genitals free and without constraint. All the time he was conscious that he had, that he carried a body. He couldn't understand how so many women could live unconscious of having those organs: their boobs and their genitals, and to hide them, even trim them down, refusing to touch them, to feel them all day long, every day. He was bereft of that sense of female reserve that usually concealed their sex. Women's sex was, or ought to be, private. Men's wasn't. Men are aware at all times of having genitals. They touch them, they keep them in one side or another of their pants.

They are always watching for possible changes in them, checking that they are noticeable, even making a show of their packet. Not being brought up a woman, Junajo lacked their scruples. Therefore he behaved like a man, and made his woman body do the same. Most of all he refused to cover his new crevice. He was so proud he would like to show everybody. He never missed a chance to flash. When crossing his legs widely, he hoped that maybe it could be noticed from below. When sitting with parted legs, lifting up his skirt in a apparently spontaneous move, maybe someone could catch a glimpse of his beloved black hole.

I have a cute cunt! was the first thing he blurted to his bed partners before getting undressed with artistic protocol. Slowly, like someone harboring a dazzling secret, he revealed it at the end, but to no avail. They didn't care. The vagina was just a place to stick the penis in. It didn't have any other value. What a big ado this broad makes of her crack, they thought. Surely it is like any other. Beautiful! they conceded jesuitically, while they introduced their blind dick into the, for them, undistinguished hole. But this hole was not like any other. It had cost him blood and tears. As Juanjo used to boast, it was a hand crafted cunt. He was irritated by the indifference displayed by some ignorant oafs. If they knew how much he had paid for it, perhaps they would change their minds. Not only it took most of his little savings, but above all, the sufferings he had to endure. He didn't want to remember.

Juanjo had not decided to have his genitals removed as yet. The idea had crossed his mind as a distant possibility but it would probably never have materialized were it not for the Moor's murder. When he was alone in the street, wanted by the police and not knowing where to go or what to do, he thought of Azucena. She liked him, and would protect him, while he searched for a solution. When Juanjo appeared, Azucena was just preparing the trip to Casablanca for the operation to remove what she owned as a man, to get rid of those obnoxious organs and recover the shape of a complete woman. The police where looking for a man, then he would become a woman. That's how he arrived in Morocco, to leave the country as a stunning knockout.

Poor Azucena had enjoyed the trip. Like so many immigrants to Catalonia she had a Andalucian grandfather, and with him she had visited the region. In Morocco, everything reminded her of it. The house patios with their fountain in the middle, the tiles, the carved counterpanes, the nail studded doors, whitewashed walls, even certain smells...They were all reminiscences.

They took advantage of the trip to make a short tour of Moroccan cities and picturesque haunts. They had visited the medinas, letting themselves be led by their guides, two rogues picked among the many who volunteered to go along for a few coins. The youngsters fought each other off for the job. They were surrounded by a swarm of sharp eyed ragamuffins, far older than their slight bodies warranted, and had difficulty in dispersing them, keeping only two as guides. The kids were keen as mustard. They spoke several languages any way they could. They addressed Juanjo in English at first, probably because of his appearance, but soon they took up Castilian with total ease. They manipulated them skillfully, pushing them along when they stopped in front of a store to take them to others were they probably got a kickback on the sales.

"Our children," observed Azucena, "are innocents compared to these. They are mentally stunted by television pap."

"Necessity sharpens your wits. These are direct relatives of Lazarillo de Tormes," said Juanjo feeling lost, like the old blind man of the novel, among all those "pícaros."

"Was Lazarillo also the name of your...the Moor you lived with"? asked Azucena.

Juanjo couldn't help a laugh. He soon repressed it, having no one to share it with. It is not fun to laugh alone. It is easier to cry. When alone, people let themselves be overcome by sadness. They manage to concentrate morbidly on their grief, grief for its own sake, for its own pain. No one cries for the grief of others but for their own, or at least, for the sorrow felt for other sorrows. Unleashed by our self pity, our pent up grief spill over liberating us, wetting handkerchiefs and pillows. This way unhappy people increase their own affiction which soon melts into tears. It is always better to be seen, but then there are people who hide to cry. But not to laugh. Laughter requires participation. Juanjo could not amuse himself with Azucena's question as he would have with his cronies. Cultural references were wasted on Azucena. She hardly had any schooling. Even so, after Juanjo told her about Lazarillo, she decided to read the book on her return home, changed fully into a woman.

Dazed, they strolled around the alleys, amidst a teeming world. In the surrounding din, they were wary of dray donkeys that made their way among the crowds no matter what. Their drivers called out with a single shout to warn the imminent presence of the beast, and the pedestrians hastily withdrew. A precarious balance was necessary not to fall among the fish, fruit, vegetables or baskets full of mint offered by sellers seated on the ground, leaning against the chipped walls of the alley. The smell of donkey dung and of the populace mixed with wafts of gardenmint, spices, herbs, the henna on the women's hair or hands, the whiff of the old merchant's pipe...Everything hit Juanjo's nose. He was as sharp to recognize the most subtle fragrances as the worst stinks. When visiting the Fez medina with Azucena, their boy guide had pointed at the tannery. The stink was noticeable already from several yards away, and he wanted to discourage them from entering. Ladies couldn't stand it, said the little rogue, accompanying his words with a gesture of pressing his nose with two fingers and then pretending to faint. At the first hint of the foul smell, Azucena withdrew. Juanjo didn't want to miss anything and he entered the place, a large square patio surrounded by multilevered arches where hides were hung to dry and where the porters were unloading more burros. On the floor, hides were piling up by the basketful. Sitting on top of the smelly mounds, some children where handling the hides without the slightest sign of revulsion. Juanjo's pituitary gland, so resistant in other occasions, could not stand it that time. How could the tanners put up with it! Would that be a question of habit? He came to ponder that maybe those people, uprooted from their own world, imigrants in busy European cities, forced to breathe factory smoke and city smog, would perhaps miss that unspeakable stench. It reminded them of their home, the same way that Juanjo found the smell of cow dung pleasant. Perhaps it was not just the smell, but the fact that it brought him back to his childhood, the holidays at the family pazo, the walks on the country lanes where the odour of dung mixed with the smell of eucalyptus, camomille and thistle, the taste of the blackberries picked on the way, and the sound of carts singing, piping away non stop.

At some crossroads, from a passer by, from a store, Juanjo breathed a familiar smell of silk, of wood, of perfume...like the many gifts the Moor had given him. He still could not believe he was dead, the more so because he never saw his corpse, except for the image given by Sabela in her hurried description of the crime. But even so, he could not believe he had been muredered that way. And now, he was there, in the Moor's world, surrounded by his people, maybe encountering some of his kin...He couldn't help but look around with certain apprehension.

Not all women, as it was generally believed, covered their faces with a veil or with an embroidered white kerchief. Some of them had their faces uncovered or covered just their heads with multicolored shawls. Or wore white wimples, like nuns. Under their long, dark and straight tunics, the slimness of some contrasted with the bulk of Berber peasant women, dressed on their voluminous red and white striped skirts, enormous white towels covering their heads as a mantle. They did not veil their faces, but wore enormous straw hats that hid them completely by slightly bowing their heads when they suspected the curiosity of onlookers, or the tourists and their cameras. Some carried their sleeping children on their hips, wrapped up on their mantles, snug on the solidity of their mother's steps.

Men's headgear showed different shapes. Some covered their heads with woollen caps, or their own shellaba's hoods, impervious to the heat. Some others wore tall, tasselled red bonnets, similar to the ones worn by robbed doctors in our universities at an inauguration. Others wore a small round skullcap, like a bishop. The models of church hierarchy were there to prove that the cradle of monasticism was oriental. The university of Fez was also older than any in the Peninsula. Maybe, thought Juanjo, that's where Spanish Ph.D's imported their attire from.

Differences in clothing and their colors were prominent, and Juanjo suspected their variation was not due to fashion, but to indicate religion, caste or social class.

They went through the markets. They were blinded by the colors of the wool yarns hanging from the top of the awnings that sheltered them from the sun. Dresses and tunics danced in their hangers, moved by invisible fingers. Juanjo bought all the tunics the Moor had refused to give him. He observed the artisans' deftly handling of their buring over gold leaf, and listened to the tinkle of the graver on the copper. His eyes fastened on the turns of the shuttle on the loom, and he was amazed by the dexterity of the artisans using their feet to hold their handiwork so that their hands would be free to work on it. He could never suspect men to be so resourceful. Many of the craftsmen were mere children. Civilization is a drag, thought Juanjo; the more advanced it is, or they say it is, the more we lose our abilities and become clumsy. Over there, with so many machines, soon we won't need hands, feet, anything, said Azucena without realizing that her defense of the natural against the artificial was at loggerheads with her presence there. Her intention was to defy nature, substituting her own God-given male organs for a hole similar to women's. She never thought of that.

Happily, eyes still fascinated by the Moroccan scene, blinded by the light, brought down by the heat and loaded with parcels they entered the clinic where their operations would take place. Azucena's enthusiasm was contagious. She abandoned herself to her fate, pure and naïve, ready to be born anew to correct the mistake of her first birth. This time, she would affirm with glee, after leaving the delivery room, it wouldn't be: it's a boy! but it's a girl! Poor thing! She never became a full woman. She never even left the operating table, having died during the operation.

It took a long time for Juanjo to find out. He never knew till he was given all Azucena's belongings upon being discharged. He was physically and morally devastated when he left the clinic. That horrible place was the rack where he had suffered the most atrocious pains he could ever believe to endure. He called his mother insistently, making the nurses smile with scorn. In his delirium Merceditas appeared, caressing him: "kiss and make it better;" rubbing Vicks Vaporub on his chest with her breezy, loving hands; blowing on the burning poultice: just a little longer, my king. He refused to open his eyes so as not to stop seeing her. He felt her fingers touching his hurting skin like a satin dress over his body in front of his bedroom mirror. It was a relief, a veil that separated him from torture. Mommy! His pains were hateful. Saint Xil was invoked in every possible way. May God spare us all we can bear, he had heard Maria's mother say once when he was a child, her daughter being sick and in pain. She was right. In his suffering, Juanjo screamed, fought, asked for death, his senses foundering. The unconcerned nurses practiced horse cures on him. Putas! Juanjo insulted them, convinced that they were doing it on purpose. The few lucid moments when his pains let up, Juanjo thought the nurses' harshness due to spit, to loathing. The same dressings, lovingly changed, with some gentleness, would be less of a martyrdom. However, they, those putas, didn't care, thought Juanjo. He couldn't understand what they said, but the tone and the sly looks transpired their disdain. For them he was a noxious maricón, a pervert who dared to defy Nature's sacred laws. He deserved punishment from heaven, and he was already getting some of it. They crossed the door in the nurses' caps he would always associate with pain, their torture instruments sharp and ready. On their lips, a cruel and sardonic smile that Juanjo was convinced was the same of the devils around Old Nick's cauldron Father Puga used to tell him about. Other times they would look like the bogey man he had been afraid of as a child. One of the nurses was from Tanger and spoke some Spanish. She airily dismissed Juanjo's complaints. Well, well, if you want

something, you must pay for it. Come on, a big man like you behaving
like that, bellyaching so, bawling...she finished with ironic tone. A man!
They are messing about with my cunt at their heart's content and they
call me a man, to hurt me more, thought Juanjo with indignation. It
served him good, to get mixed up with Saracenes. It was not enough the
Moor, that cabrón who complicated his life even after death. And
now...Juanjo's revulsion grew with the torture that was driving him
crazy.

Even so, the nurses' cruelty did not reach the extreme to tell him
right away about Azucena's death. They kept it under wraps until the
moment he was discharged, fully recuperated and could abandon that
cursed place. He cried like a Magdalene.

He had to go on crying. For Azucena, for himself, for whomever.
One of the good things of being a woman, Juanjo found out, was that one
could cry without restraint or shame. Juanjo became a crybaby. All of
a sudden it was as if a dam had burst, and all the suppressed tears of his
life ran out of control. He had always laughed more than cried. Now
it was the opposite.

It took a long time for Azucena to be erased from his mind. In his
dreams he looked like a saint, one of those martyrs dead for their faith.
With a pure white tunic and sleepy eyes he walked across heaven
carrying her balls on a silver platter, like St. Lucy her eyes.

It took him as long to recuperate from his body wounds as of his
sadness. He tried to forget while trying to become a woman. He had
adapt to his new appearance, to the new organs. It was not only a
question of being a woman, but of being acknowledged as such. The
perception and behavior of others would pass judgement on him as a
woman. That's why he labored so hard to act the part while trying to
overcome the changes on his body. Being a woman on the outside was
easier than assuming femininity, embody all that silent and intimate
plasticity. He had to get used to his new relationship with men. He had
to transform his sexual proclivities, keeping them low, changing them
into tenderness, sweetness, affection, as it befitted a real woman. He
should never take the initiative. Better let them in charge of the sexual
act, take over the helm. And all that had to be accepted as something
biological, natural. He had to find yet his own niche. On previous
relationships, when he was a man, intercourse was not always egalitarian.
Sometimes, the customer held certain privileges of use and possession,
but those were considered more like a momentarily concession. The

weaker part could think: I am playing the mother, but I am not one, eh? Like you, I have balls, virility, power. I am a person; and at other moments he would behave as such. But being a woman you couldn't. You were never a subject. Your submission was natural. Women's nature was to exit for others. Juanjo tried to accept this, to become mother, matter. He couldn't desire but had to want to be desired. He could not indulge in rebellious thoughts. If he wanted to be a woman, men were the ones who made you so. Otherwise, he would be unfinished, incomplete.

For Juanjo, born and raised proud, a Valladares, it was a difficult process. To bite a rejoinder in the tongue, to hide the arrow ready to hit the bullseye of discourse; to dwaddle on ellipses that dismantled all his logical assumptions drove him crazy, made him roll his eyes till he became cross-eyed. He would strive to conform. He couldn't fail in his plans to become a woman, to join another world. He had to materialize the mirage. More over, he had to invent another mirror of his self.

The moment had come to make his mark as an actress, to take on the job he had learned as a child, and that Merceditas had dreamed about. It was a way to be worthy of her, to fulfill her expectations.

The first step was to pick a new name, a woman's name to answer to, to introduce herself by. The choice was not easy. It was really curious that parents never seemed to have any trouble to choose their children's name. Normally they had one ready well before the baby was born. The choice obeyed to several reasons, but physical appearance was not one. Nobody can tell how a baby will look, or what will be its fate. So when they grow up, people have to put up with a name that maybe it's displeasing to them, or does not fit their image. Sometimes it even contradicts their appearance. A Blanca may to totally dark; Preciosa may be ugly; Felicidad could be extremely unhappy; Digna, a woman with a life full of indignity.

Were everybody allowed to choose their names personally, it would be a complicated choice, just as it was for Juanjo. He didn't like delicate names, like Fina or Delgadina. Besides, it was not only the meaning of the name to bear in mind. The sound of the word itself was even more important. For example, Silvia or Luisa, with their sibilant, sharp syllables, and slippery, soft sibilants were more appropriate for slight, slender creatures, not for a big woman like Juanjo. He thought other vibrant, well rounded names, more appropriate: Roberta, Ramona...After much shuffling around he eventually settled for Rafaela. The name had a hint of virility and strength in the Rafa, and of sweetness in the ela. Besides, the ending was also very Galician, like Sabela.

With the new name Juanjo, Rafaela, dreamed of playing creditably all the great heroines of tragedy. He saw himself on stage like Juliet, like Antígona...He was convinced there were no actresses in the whole country greater than him. Of women of real consequence, capable of arousing great passions, there weren't any left. They were not big enough. On the contrary, she, Rafaela, who would not admire her! For instance in *Yerma*, a play that fitted her like a glove, the yearn to be a woman, the complete woman spilling out her guts, was his own. Yerma was a little bit herself. And on top of it, she knew how to recite. *Yerma* was a play to belt out without a syllable being lost. Really, no one cared about the text in the theater anymore, Juanjo complained. It seemed as if words were of no consequence, only stage props mattered. That was true. Complicated sets, revolving stages, different techniques, lights' play, fabulous costumes...All ready for the big show. But on stage people milled about from one end to another as if playing blindman's buff. Let's have movement. Dehumanized puppets more in line with beings made of cardboard. Most of the time Juanjo left the theater disappointed, thinking that should Rafaela herself be out there, she would make the audience stir, cry and laugh, get into the character's skin, suffer with her. That was to be an actress; the rest were paper dolls.

He made the tour of all theaters, trying to get an audition from the producers. Nothing. He could not get a part. Only the girlfriends, the daughters, or the lovers of someone would, muttered Juanjo. It was a world tight as a drum. And critics contributed to close the circle even more.

Juanjo was really good at theater. He was a full time actor. Only, instead of personifying other people, he always played himself out. But this nonstop performance prevented him to think clearly. He was good, and he attracted the public. People around him were thrilled. They clapped, they laughed at his jokes. He was totally at ease on life's stage, sure of his appeal. That's why he never stopped to consider that he had a surfeit of faculties that were not recognized by society, and therefore wasted. He had all the potential of a winner and yet he was a failure. Luckily, with the zest of permanent exposure, he had little spare time to think about this. He lacked dedication even for resentment.

Juanjo got a job at a nightclub. Between musical shows Rafaela recited. He didn't go for the love songs he had learned from his mother, but for long, dramatic poems telling about unhappy childhoods, mothers dead young of consumption, passions, jealousy, unrequited love...The sight of Rafaela's radiant blond beauty, dressed in black silk offseting the full curves of her body, her silicone breasts spilling out of the neckline, all that gave a surrealistic touch to the scene. To recite those lines with a tragically broken voice was or could be joke in that place. It was logical to think that the impresario's sense of humor and opportunity had hired Rafaela for that reason: to make the customers explode in guffaws before the rhymed calamities she declaimed so seriously, vastly engrossed by her own performance. But no matter what, she never forgot her body. Rafaela was never unaware of her body, the rounded forms, the newly acquired organs, and that was one of her big successes. When people looked at her, they could not help being mesmerized by her figure. The permanent fixation Rafaela felt for herself was contagious to those around her.

Whatever might be the intention of the club owners, the result was that those patrons in search of a good time, those who went to look at her as merchandise, or to laugh about her charms, were soon held in sway by her act. When they announced: The great dramatic actress Rafaela! and she stepped defiantly on the boards, here is my body!, the catcalls, the jokes, the jeers erupted riotously. But as soon as she began to recite, to tell the story, rolling out sufferings and misfortunes, all those pitiless and scornful big oafs began to melt, and did what they could to hide behind their drinks the tears held back in their eyes. Rafaela in turn, let big drops fall over her prominent cheekbones like a perennial fountain. We know that she had acquired a great ability to cry. She gave the impression of getting herself into the dramatic stories she told till the point of living them out. The truth was that Juanjo cried for other reasons. At those moments he remembered his own grief for Azucena's death, his mother's absence, the lost happiness of childhood, his own failures. That was the trick for his tears. His big blue eyes filled to the brim, the tears ran down his face, and the men in the audience fought to hide their own emotions. When she finished, they clapped enthusiastically, immediately recovering their wits and mastering the situation. In unison, they returned to the cries, the brutal compliments, the wolf whistles. The tears hidden on their tearducts, held back during the act, could run out now easily, mixed with the jeers and the jokes. Water me with those tears, crying woman. I am hot as an oven! I would gladly make you cry, but for other reasons! If you fuck the way you cry, you are priceless! Do you want me to show you where my tears come from, hot pants? Thus they rowdily cried, those sensitive guys.

Crying woman. So great was his ability to cry that he was giving the nickname "Rafaela la Llorona," or simply "Llorona." If the impresarios thought the nickname would mean the demystifying of the act, or that the comical would triumph over the tragedy, they were wrong again. Even the music announcing her appearance on stage, the famous Mexican song, "La Llorona," sang along by the audience, did not prevent Juanjo's tears to move even the stones.

The nightclub act, however, became stale with time. Other faces, other bodies, came to take over. These were times of change. People continuously requested something new, quality be damned. He was soon out of a job. He only had gigs in the summer, in nightclubs of the East coast, or at the Costa del Sol. His savings, the money hoarded to start a modest business, were spent on the operation. He saw himself once more in the streets, exposed to humiliation and dependency.

In his former experience, in those bitter moments when he felt himself despised by inconsiderate people, he could think: they are doing this to me because I am a maricón, a social leper. If I were a woman, they would treat me with more respect. In this, he had stopped deluding himself. The scorn of those who bought women was not any less. Besides, they considered that the mere fact of being a woman had to be proven in certain behaviors of submission and service. Because she could not respond faithfully to these stereotypes, Rafaela had skirmishes all the time. At times, when she was feeling really down, she had the urge to tell the others: I am a man like you. I am a subject.

Sometimes she hated, yes, hated being a woman. He even felt rage against women. Could it be true what they said, that women are thus by nature, carrying submission in their genes? Was their behavior genetic or acquired? Juanjo turned it around in his head. He knew that, no matter how much he looked like a woman, genetically he was still a man. His chromosomes had not changed. Cultural traits could be acquired by imitation, by learning, but biological ones...How could he distinguish one from the other?

When he left the clinic he had been determined to learn to be a woman. What he didn't know is that there would come times when he would refuse to be one. He rebelled against female submission. He could not understand how women consented to it, if consented they did.

Where they born with an inclination to submit? Was this an inborn thing or was it rather life experience, their own and other women's, what had made them to obey?

Chapter 6

"It is not true that it's inborn," denied Chicha hotly. "You live in such sordid atmosphere, among people so degraded that it has made you judge all women by the same standards. But, as you can see, we are not all like that. There are women who revolt, many of us, and we are growing in number every day. We value independence and personal dignity above everything," stated Chicha smugly, lifting up absentmindedly her glasses that tended to slide down her small nose.

They had the afternoon free and their friends would not arrive till the evening. These moments of confidences. But Rafaela was sorry already for the turn taken by the conversation. She was shaken by Chicha's harsh stance. She usually didn't mince words. "Yes, in that respect some of you are like men," answered Rafaela.

"What?" snapped Chicha without letting her finish.

"I mean that some of you show a real manly behavior, male pride," explained Rafaela.

"What do you mean, male? Pride can also be female's" she started pushing her glasses up her nose. "You are full of prejudice. Not all women are like the ones you know, and not all men behave towards women like those savages you have encountered. Some men are more civilized. My co-workers..."

"Yeah, yeah," cut in Rafaela. "Don't go on. Sure, we know men different ways, just as you say, different times and circumstances. But honey," and she adopted a knowing leer, "you would be surprised to see the behavior of those considerate fellows when they can abuse someone. When they are at a place where other rules apply. I tell you even more: I do not know it from experience, since I haven't been a woman for very long, but older hookers are fuming. My friend Paca, who has been at it for many years, tells me that customers have been rather peeved lately. She blames the feminists. It is the fault of those dykes, as she puts it indignantly, that men take it on us harder than ever before."

"How silly!" said Chicha with a dismissing shrug.

"No, seriously," replied Rafaela, embracing her knees with her hands and resting her head pensively on them. "Since they see themselves deprived of privileges in certain situations, men take advantage from others as much as they can. It makes sense, no?"

"Bah! There is always time to back down. In truth, they haven't lost many privileges," contradicted Chicha. "But yes, the number of those of us who are not at their beck and call is growing more and more," she conceded smugly, lifting up the cup to her lips.

Rafaela and Chicha drank mint tea sitting on a couch against the wall, among sharp colored pillows. Everything was happy and bright around them. There is little furniture in the white room. Facing the couch some pine shelves hold books, a record player, dolls and many ceramic objects. On the wall above the couch there is a big poster of Virginia Woolf.

Rafaela stretched her legs and set the cup on the round table. She goes back to the pillows, arranging carefully her embroidered, wide tunic around her. Her unruly blond curls are plaited and clubbed by a pin of tiny roses which intensifies her fresh, youthful appearance. The fragrance of lavender increases the feeling of freshness radiated by her. She is not wearing any make up; she has the air of a Nordic peasant girl. She no longer cared for those warm, heavy perfumes or the vampy dresses. But she still objected to underwear. She did not need a bra, and as for panties, not much either. At home, and whenever she could, she wore nothing under her tunic or her jeans. Chicha shared her desire of freedom, of not feeling constraint or oppression in any way. She never wore a bra either. But Chicha did not share Rafaela's conscience of carrying a body, feeling it at every moment.

"You, feminists," said Rafaela, "are a social élite. Most women do not accept your arguments. Neither have they the possibility to escape their miserably inferior role. Your theories are for the chosen few, for those who can allow themselves the luxury of being proud. Dignity is something that the poor, the wretched, and the humble, cannot afford," insisted Rafaela with the conviction of having lived through it.

"You simplify far too much." replied Chicha. "Pride and dignity do not belong with the rich or the poor. There can be proud poor and cowed rich. You know very well that some rich wives are ornamental objects, attractive and well groomed like some kind of deluxe, private hookers. Those women have a personality as debased and impoverished as the streetwalkers you are familiar with," affirmed Chicha emphatically.

"Even so, they have a much better life," rebuked Rafaela.

"That's beside the point," contested Chicha. "We were talking about pride and dignity, of the possibility of being truly independent."

"I know you don't like me to say it, my dove," Rafaela softened her voice while caressing Chicha's hair. Undoubtedly finding the gesture too paternalistic, Chicha pulled away as if pricked. "Yes," she stopped Chicha's rejoinder with her hand, "the only ones who have certain autonomy regarding men are you lesbians, since you do not need them for love or sex..."

"We?" asked Chicha ironically.

"Well, myself included," conceded Rafaela. "The others, no matter how financially secure, are always trapped. When in love, they put up with everything. And then there are the problems of their sex. Either they become pregnant or they stuff themselves with pills or they travel to London for abortions. Trapped, I tell you," and Rafaela lifted her chin from her knees and faced Chicha's gaze unflinchingly. "Why do you think I could get out? Because they could not impregnate me...That gave me certain security, certain power over them..."

"You could escape because you found me," said Chicha firmly, kissing her curls and cuddling up to her.

Rafaela stretched her legs and reached for her teacup on the table. Chicha got up to place a new Janis Joplin record on, and sat down again next to her. Rafaela let Chicha lean on her and rest her head on her belly. Chicha's head, with her short hair and sidelocks, settled snugly on her lap. Rafaela yanked off her glasses and bent down to kiss her. She looked into Chicha's porcelain eyes, still alive now but which would become blurred over the years due to her glasses. Her eyes looked at Rafaela with charming defiance before they both laid down and began to kiss in earnest.

Rafaela could play for hours with her lips and tongue. Since she discovered the pleasure of kissing she had become a smoocher. She mused upon this. It was not that Chicha kissed better than others, but rather her unflagging delight in kissing. Kissing developed as an independent activity, and end to itself that might or might not have continuity. In her former life, for herself and for those who kissed her, kissing was a prerequisite to fuck. She felt their impatience, their haste to finish that dull ritual. They glued their lips to hers, cold as a Medusa's, while all the time their pricks burned between their legs. There were others who inserted their hard tongues in her mouth, forcibly denouncing the penis they were dying to stick in. Perhaps it was not always thus, but Juanjo or Rafaela felt the rush on the kisses she gave and received. Now she had discovered the pleasure of kissing. Without hurry, without...Other things would inevitably follow...but nothing was fixed beforehand.

She had become pensive and absent.

"What's wrong?" asked Chicha.

"I was thinking of something you may like. I don't know as a person...but as a kisser I am autonomous. Kisses are independent things."

"Not at all. At this moment they are dependant on me," said Chicha pulling down her neck and bringing her closer.

Chicha enjoyed pressing slightly on her yielding lips which pressed back in turn. Her wet tongue licked them softly, stopping at the corners, searching for a little opening where to insert the tip, sharp as a cobra's. Another mouth, hot and humid, opened up to meet hers, a meat-eating plant ready to devour. The tongue entered slowly the deep cave where another tongue rose to the meet, silent and playful at first like the spark of a young fire. Their forces clashed on a live, fleshy swordplay, a game of impulse and inconsequence where the will to win yielded easily to defeat and abandon. Under their tongues their teeth play like piano keys, a melody that goes back to the lips biting softly and letting sighs of fulfillment release the passion that runs from their half closed mouths to their thirsty innards. When Rafaela came to that point, Chicha no longer existed. There was nothing outside herself. She felt her own breath return like an echo, invading everything deep inside, passion knocking at the walls of her chest. She felt pleasure gone only to turn back. The other mouth was her own, just like in the mirror in her mother's bedroom.

Chicha insisted on extricating her from her ecstasy, bringing her back adroitly to reality. She was as uninhibited in sex as in life. She was as determined in controversy and argument as in her caresses and sexual touch. Enticing and sure of herself, poised like a seagull on the rocks, like a raven on a wheat field, and with the same purpose, she took possession of her body, Rafaela's body. Chicha's strength was uncanny. Like a passionate eel, she would coil around her solid legs, clinging to her in a rhythmic and humid dance that made mud out of Rafaela's belly. Melting under the pressure of Chicha's intense thrust, collapsing in tears, cries and sweat, she felt her own body spurred like a bolting mare's. With triumphant screams Chicha dragged her on to a mysterious abyss from where they both returned changed into a mass of round forms that preserved, like clinging cobwebs, the pleasure running out of their pores which their embrace did not let escape. Their sight, coming again to focus with their recovering breaths, renewed their pleasure. At that time, the lovers stood in wonder of the mysterious roses they had just gathered. They looked at each other. Chicha's breasts, her nipples wishing to perforate hers; her belly, her clitoris that she recognized and caressed as her own...There was the mirror. Once more there was the likeness.

How strange life is, she thought caressing lightly the other's head. I started off with a woman and end up with another. Perhaps that was it, the search of femininity, what she had pursued all along her troubled life. Now she felt like a woman among women. Perhaps her mistake was wanting to be a woman, a complete woman, despite the sacrifice endured to achieve it, the torture of the transforming process. Men did not care for femininity. Only women understood women.

She took account of her lovers. None had loved her. Not even that pitiful old man who paid for her apartment in order to sleep with her once a week. Oh, he was a real softie. He drooled about his little granddaughter's school party. His son's promotion to major, albeit his youth, was a real source of pride to him. But he did not love Rafaela the same way. At least he was a gentleman, soft spoken, and he did not mistreat her. Other men, however, came to take their frustrations on her body, on what she was.

Now she believed that to be a woman was to reconcile herself to see men as the rest did. They had to nurse them like understanding mothers with consoling, bountiful bosoms. Maybe that was what he lacked, the feeling of motherhood. He never had it. He had felt desire, he still did, for his own mother, but he never wanted to be a mother. Since he was not a mother and would never want to be one, it was difficult to assume the maternal role with men, to overlook their mischief as with children, their caprices, their tantrums...He succeeded or thought he had to see, think, conceive like a woman...Conceive mentally, but not physically. He was unable to bear children.

He had been able to tolerate his disgust thanks to his imagination, the daydreaming his mother had taught him since he was a child. Fantasy was his ally, his best friend as he could not find any other in real life. His mind could rise above all that filth. It was able to change a loud mouth into a prince. Obscene words became poetry, clumsy hands changed into velvet handles. The sordid rented hotel room became a palace with a canopied bed. The raucous cries into his ears sounded like a Mozart sonata, and the sweat drops sliding down his body could be the transparent waters of a brook. Alcoholic breath could carry the perfumes of a pazo's garden, and the suffocating weight of fat bellies on his body might seem like heady mountain air blowing on his face. That's the way it was. He abandoned his body as if it were a stranger's. He escaped from it, soaring away to places of infinite delight. He was able to retrieve his body later, cleansed and unscathed, for himself, or rather herself, in order to enjoy it like no other could. He saw himself as long ago; beautiful; kissing his own lips on his mother's mirror.

Self love, the self adoration that had possessed him all his life became increasingly weak. At times he grew tired of loving himself, of the fall into the pit of loneliness. He came to disregard the desire of being a woman, forgetting the self control needed to behave like one. He had already guessed that he would only become a woman if he were loved as such. Love would make him a woman, to be a woman. To be, yes. He came often to think of his mother, the only one to love him wholly, all the time. He should never have left her. He had only been happy with her. She accepted and loved him. He didn't have to act a part: being himself was enough for her. After he left his mother, all had been a bad joke, a theatrical effort, a need to act on a hostile stage only to feel failure after each performance. Since he left his mother, he mused, no one had ever treated him like a person. He had been a ghost, a puppet. Cock or cunt alike, he was not a person anymore.

When he met Chicha he was on edge. All of a sudden another world opened up: other women. After his operation, Rafaela was surrounded by women, but women who belonged, according to Chicha, to the suffering bevy of those who lived only for men's sake. They were always talking about men, who appeared prominently in their conversations. They hated them, loved them, adored them, cursed them...But they were the center of their conversations occupying their minds entirely.

Now with Chicha, Rafaela became aware of another reality: that of women who, rather than being preoccupied with being women, wanted to be persons above all. That could save her. She concentrated happily on becoming a new person, moving in circles like a star in the sky to remake herself and the universe. Not to have essence, beginning or end. To be fulfilled, to reinvent oneself and to love, to love another woman.

After Araceli, his wife, he never had sex with another woman. With Araceli he had tried to imitate more or less lessons learned at the movies, from novels or during conversations with his adolescent friends. It was a failure. He wanted to be romantic, a seducer, a loving boyfriend, a perfect husband...A total washout. Now, again with a woman, he had to learn another lesson, the more the difficulty since there were no models to go by like before.

Sometimes, when he was with Chicha, he couldn't help to think of his severed penis. He made an effort to erase the thought. Besides, with Chicha it would have been useless. He had to strive to love her the way she wanted, as a woman. But it was not always easy, and the ghost of what he had left behind in Casablanca haunted him with stubborn disquiet while they were together.

He knew he was walking on quicksand, and was never sure his behavior was appropriate. He was afraid, terribly afraid of speaking. For the first time since he left his mother he felt cuddled, treated lovingly within a harmonious environment. He was scared to lose that.

There was also the new experience of sharing: a home, shopping for groceries, cooking...Chicha was a hospital nurse. Rafaela cared for two young girls while their mother went to work. At home there were always friends of Chicha. They were all like a big family where Rafaela represented one of Chicha's follies. They tolerated Rafaela as such. They knew Chicha was afraid of nothing: she was a steamroller capable of defying all of Nature's laws. She lived on perpetual motion, with bubbling energy. She seemed to run the world on a hidden string. People around her became puppets even without meaning to. She had met Rafaela one gaudy night when entering a single bar with a lively bunch of cronies. On spotting her she had told her friends, what a dish! What eyes! Too hot to handle, they had warned her. But no one could challenge Chicha with impunity.

Her affair with Rafaela had started as a game. Rafaela held on to Chicha as a lifeline. And now there she was. Chicha's friends put up with her, but clearly for them she didn't belong there. They could not understand Chicha's extravagance, and they thought it had lasted far too long.

She knew it was bound to happen sooner or later. She had embarked with Chicha on a trip, and was happy cruising along. But ships fatally must come to port some time. Rafaela knew it from the beginning, but wanted to forget and make the trip last as long as possible.

Ships return to home waters. Another woman appeared in Chicha's life; a same sex companion with identical ideas and plans.

Rafaela's body was again questioned and rejected. Always that controversial body. Always the conflict of true likeness.

Chicha's cruelty, even wrapped up on female logic, was not lesser than all the others.'

"I can't! Ours was a flash in the pan, a folly," exploded Chicha. "It had to end up badly. I like women, you know."

"And what am I?" asked Rafaela flabbergasted.

"You are a man," said Chicha with conviction.

Like an echo, Rafaela heard his father's voice when he drove him out of his home. You are not a real man, you are not a true man...Other voices came to him: Mistress Widow Roquefort!, cried his friends. Then he heard the hateful Moor's taunts: you are only half woman. A man doesn't cry, come on, jeered the evil Moroccan nurses. Their harsh voices trampled him down carrying their verdict. Aie! How different women's hands are! said the mother of the two babies Rafaela took care of. Rafaela had read the ad in the paper looking for a baby sitter. Chicha had encouraged her to apply. But I never cared for kids, I never knew how to handle them, protested Rafaela. She thought of her own son, the child she never bothered with, the one she seldom had seen on visits, more was the pity now. A pediatrician friend of Chicha provided some makeshift training. Rafaela practiced with dolls before she went to apply. Very clean, with a very "Little house on the prairie" look on her floral dress. Rafaela looked at the girls, how cute, identical as two peas...Their mother watched her enchanted. How different women's hands are! she said. A young man came for the job, you know, the mother explained. Sweet Jesus, I don't care how many classes he has taken, she went on accusingly, I won't leave my babies in a man's hands for the world. Not even my husband. I hardly let him touch then. He may hurt them with those clumsy hands. This is not a man's job; only women's. I only have to see how you hold them...It's different. You have children, right? No, lied Rafaela. It doesn't matter. Women have it in their blood; we are born with that gift. Even though some don't have children, we are all mothers. She looked at her. Besides, you can still have them, she concluded encouragingly.

And now Chicha passed sentence: You are a man.

"Look at me!" asked Rafaela showing her flesh. "This is a woman's body."

"Perhaps. But it is fake. Deep inside you are still a man. You think like a man. When you touch me, I feel a man's hand; when you caress me, it is a man's skin. I have tried, but I cannot get over it. Your desire is male desire. You will never want me as a woman, as your equal," concluded Chicha.

Juanjo noticed how Rafaela, the woman he carried inside, was being destroyed, broken in a million pieces. His pain was physical, inciding on those female organs that were now his, the more so because it was being inflicted by a woman.

"Wake up!" warned Chicha somewhat cynically. "You are totally carried away by an impossible dream. You don't really like women but men. If you had desired women, you wouldn't have become a transsexual. If women made you tick, you would have remained a man. Can't you see how absurd it all is? Yours was a big mistake," went on Chicha, reaffirming her argument while pushing her glasses up her nose. "So much work for nothing."

"Yes. So much work for nothing," repeated Rafaela stunned.

"Admit that you wanted to become a woman for men's sake, not for women's or even for my own," insisted Chicha.

"No," denied Rafaela, "I did not become a woman for any one but to be myself."

"To be yourself?" argued Chicha. "You don't need operations for that. You only have to accept who you are and face life with guts. That's the only honorable way. But on the contrary, you wanted to be an object. You carved out that hole for them, so men could fuck you at leisure."

"How wrong you are!" replied Rafaela bitterly, showing some spine for the first time. "Hole for hole, most of them prefer the other, I can assure you."

"Then why?" insisted Chicha.

"I wanted to be a woman. Totally. A woman to everybody. To be seen as female, treated as female," he begged holding Chicha's hand imploringly between his.

"You were rather silly, then. Look at your choice!," said Chicha nervously, withdrawing her hand. "When women are born, they have a destiny fixed by their sex. We either have to accept it or revolt against our female condition, the marginality that condemns us. But no man wants to lose the privileges he holds due to the mere fact of being born a man. No man wants to be a woman. I wish the opposite were true."

"There you are!" concluded Juanjo. "I chose to be a woman. I wanted to, understand? I have more merit than those of you who were born women; more that those who want to be men, who reject being women and suffer from penis' envy."

"Here comes old Freud!" cuts Chicha sarcastically.

"I know nothing about Freud. I am not so knowledgeable as you hard-line feminists. I never said a word in your meetings...But I learned something. Among other things, that famous quote of that Frenchie, Simone whatever. She said very clearly that a woman is not born but she becomes one. Eh?" argues Rafaela triumphantly. "What do you have to say to that? Was she wrong? I became one!"

"You misunderstand completely the meaning of the quote," contradicted Chicha. "It is just the opposite of what you think. It means that women are not constrained by nature; our marginality is social. We are not born slaves; it is society that makes it so. Therefore, we can liberate ourselves."

"I chose freely to become a woman," insisted Juanjo.

"But one is not a woman only for having some fake female sex organs. Being a woman means more than tits, calves, cunt..."

Being a woman is to be pitiless like you, thought Rafaela, but didn't say it, stunned by Chicha's phlegmatic, severe sexual revindications. In the heat of the argument, Chicha's glasses slid down all the time, and she was compelled to restore them in place, wrinkling up her nose on her habitual gesture. Rafaela looked at her and for the first time, that tic which she had always thought charming, seemed hateful to her. She saw Chicha as a ridiculous monkey, aping gestures, allowing herself to rule what was not to be a woman. In her life Rafaela had met violence and rage, but never scorn as inhuman as that young woman's.

Again his sexual body was being questioned. Another stage out of so many in his contested, broken personality. He couldn't get a hold of his senses. He felt chaos in his mind, breakdowns, shortcircuits, alternate frequencies. He was in the void, blinded, without seeing clearly where, when, how or why.

And Chicha, so sure of herself, orating. Rafaela looked at her without seeing her, like in a fog, far away. She didn't reply. Tears were choking her words. They were the same tears she would spill over as a waterfall, over the gossamer tunics, the plaid blouses, the designer jeans stuffed in a bag. She picked up her things. The brightness of the house, the whiteness of the walls had always made her happy. Today everything had the pallor of death. There, in that house, she would have been safe. She only needed a crumb of tenderness to compose her own self, so battered by life's turns. And strangely, she was leaving the place even more destroyed than before. Her likeness was not accepted. Pain, disappointment prevented her indignation to emerge, but she knew that she could blame Chicha for her difference the same way. Chicha was not like other women. She broke the rules, she also defied nature. Nevertheless, she rejected Rafaela's difference. The guardians of order are everywhere. They can even fix the degree of disorder among the disorderly, the margins on marginality. Every human being carries an inquisitor within.

She readied herself to leave that house, discarding her lifesaver without a murmur. After all he was a Valladares, and kept still some shreds of family pride. He realized that he had not thought of himself as a he for a long time. He had not thought of himself as a man. At first, he could not understand what could unchain that reaction now. Perhaps Chicha's cruelty, a woman's, made him come to despise all her sex. Perhaps Chicha was right, and it was true he didn't want to be a woman, an inferior, a witch like her. More than that, he decided, what caused his permanence in the masculine was the sense of pride, the Valladares' family nobility. The lessons of Chicha and her friends had not succeeded to eradicate the private conviction, perhaps the prejudice, that pride and dignity were not a woman thing. Juanjo had assumed those traits to be male's. With the exception of Merceditas, Valladares' pundonor was a mark of their virility. His mother's memory poisoned all his wounds. No one, man or woman, could take his mother's place in his heart. For a moment he hated his female attributes, this woman's body which prevented him to appear in front of Merceditas, get on his knees and kiss the lines time must have drawn on her face. He could not imagine his mother growing old. He discarded a thought that created such painful response in him. His mother would be eternally young in his eyes. Reality would not betray her image for he would never see her again. Merceditas would always be the shepherdess with the long blond tresses, singing the medieval cantigas; the conniving confident who put ideas into his head. She was a Valladares and walked firmly on Lugo's streets in state, as if stepping on soft carpets under her feet, the feet of a great lady.

He had not been to a place like this, a gay bar, for a very long time. Even upon entering he already noticed several changes. There was more light, the view was more clear. These places, thought Juanjo, used to be darker and more sordid before. The idea of the forbidden, of sin, had lurked in every shady corner. Deceit hid in glances, in clandestine touchings. Forbidden encounters had a certain charm; however now it was all changed by permissiveness. People also behaved differently. The younger generation did not mind necking or kissing openly. The older ones, the queers, still kept the reserve of older times.

The intense, expressive glances still electrified the air like as in a silent movie. The bystanders, elbows resting on the counter, or leaning on columns with a glass on their hands, adopted a nonchalant or cautious stance. Their anxiety was noticeable. Their movements were more fit for a theatrical performance. Next to the seasoned ones, the disappointed veterans, hopeful newcomers showed their anticipation for a first experience. Only the crazy, hyperactive queers lightened the atmosphere. They danced disjointedly as mannequins, adlibbing in front of the impromptu audience. They scampered about needlessly, making themselves conspicuous, jostling passive drinkers, rattling their bones around, rigid in their masculinity. Rafaela felt certain pity for the exhibitionist eagerness displayed. How well she understood them! Those comedians were her people once. Were she in a different mood, she would probably join them. Who would see her moving around the dance floor, offering her alabaster breasts for public scrutiny!

Today he had tried dressing like a man again. He felt so strange! It was impossible. He wanted to play the mariquita but Rafaela defeated any plumes. She was simply a lady dressed in man's clothing. He had put on a musky perfume, full of male seduction. He searched at drugstores for his mother's "Oriental Woods," but couldn't find it. It was no longer sold. So much the better. He was glad not to find it afterwards. The fragrance would bring a sorrow he was not willing to endure. Smells had for Juanjo an evocative quality that overwhelmed any other sensation. Bloodhound nose, his mother called him when, as a child, he could smell from downstairs the dessert that María, the cook, was fixing in the kitchen on the third floor. Aroma gave him more pleasure than taste. He smelled drink and food before tasting. On some occasions, taste betrayed the smell, meaning it was not up to par with the promised aroma.

He had arrived at the hangout in despair, searching for his origins. The image of Miguel Anxo, the young man who had unleashed a new sexual force in him, was on his mind all day. He wanted to see him again. He would be there; with all the habituals to his Lugo parties. He wanted to see them, to recognize them. That short guy looked like

Naparreto Jarsía. The oaf sitting across, Shameless Doris; the little brown one, Moor-Eater Lili. And also others; Firefly, Good-for-Nothing...the whole gang. Only one was missing; the Widow Roquefort. Was he superseded by Rafaela? Juanjo didn't know anymore. The only thing he knew was that he was not the same. He didn't have Juanjo's eyes. Everything around him was strange. He didn't belong. Where did he? He remembered Chicha; you are a man, you like men...The words beat on his brain insistently. Was it true? He was here to find out.

Through the mirror he was able to pick up one customer, a big guy with a mustache, looking rather passé. The man wore a print shirt like his own, not to disguise his boobs but his paunch, bloated by perhaps too many beers that had made his figure rather ugly. Rigid, with a drink in his hand, he airily pretended not to care, but Juanjo, knew, and who else would fool him on those tricks! that he was ogling him through the mirror. I have to try, he repeated while he played the game and started the closing in. His powers of seduction couldn't fail him. And they didn't.

He found himself soon enough in that oaf's room even though he ignored his name. Details were inconsequential. Any effort to start a conversation was cut short. The guy didn't mind niceties. He had no time to loose. Shall we have a drink at my place? he suggested. He had his car right there. He lived near the Roman bridge, across the river. A foul smelling river, full of industrial waste, plastic bottles, debris, noxious foam which had lost its whiteness...Even though, when crossing the bridge, the moonlight pierced the black clouds which had unloaded tons of water all day, illuminating the river. Looking at the mirroring waters, Juanjo let himself be touched by the landscape, the gloomy night, the swollen river he heard. The river came back to life, recovering for a moment the initial purity and force of its youth. Its waters carried the freshness of the high mountains of its birth, the lymph of the forests bathed by its course, the fury of the hostile stones of the riverbed. The river's rearing, angry look, rose above the pollution, as if rebelling against the human refuse dumped on its waters, angrily forcing all the detritus gather and beat against the stone pillars of the Roman bridge.

Like flotsam and jetsam, Juanjo let himself go by a blind impulse, like an unconscious river, while Chicha's words stuck on his gut. He preferred to blend into the uncertainty of that moonlight, still stronger than the apocalyptic clouds that threatened to extinguish the light of his reasoning.

The whole thing was a failure. The awful queer looked at his naked body as an irritating and uncomfortable object. His beloved body, so contemplated in mirrors, recreated, caressed, transformed; that body he valued as the purest marble, had become now a noxious beast, a repugnant mass in the eyes of that brute. Juanjo had felt often, or had been made to feel, a pleasurable object, but never a repulsive thing like at that moment. He felt his body go to pieces, pulverized like a handful of dust. He covered it quickly with his clothes like someone hiding something unspeakable from view.

"Yeah, better put some clothes on," he said picking up his drink as if the session was over. "I like men; I think that's obvious," he stated angrily.

"I am a man," Juanjo had still the courage to remonstrate. Look at my ID," and he made sign of showing the old card.

"Sex is not a question of ID's," dismissed the other.

"Of what, then?" asked Juanjo.

"Of having what it takes," he replied with realistic conviction.

"Sexual identity is something else. It is not the same as body reality," Juanjo repeated Chicha's words like an automaton. "The important thing is what is inside, the deep leanings..."

"Look, spare me your philosophies at this time of the night," said the other furious. "I have wasted enough time on you."

"You must believe I am a man," insisted Juanjo obsessively, more for himself than for his companion.

"Perhaps you are. But what I want is a big cock, understand?"

"How gross!" exclaimed Juanjo.

"Where are you coming from? What a square!" He heaped his scorn on Juanjo. "Such a big body and so squeamish!"

Juanjo put on his coat, hurtling blindly down the stairs. Foul insults rained upon him. Show off your cunt some more, see if you get lucky...They bounced off his empty head, his disjointed body. They killed the woman; they also murdered the man he carried inside. No he was nobody.

The moon was definitively hidden behind clouds, black and big as somber castles. Perhaps if the clear beam of the mysterious moonlight had not disappeared carrying away the beauty of the landscape, destroying the magic that hid the polluted river, the stunted trees by the riverside, the crumbling houses beyond...Perhaps if the moon hadn't left, it would have given Juanjo some strength to go on living, even if only to imagine all the beauty that never existed. But no. The moon was gone. All became definitely sordid and Juanjo was to play his last part, death. Leaning on the bridge's parapet he hardly saw the refuse that the unfeeling river piled up under the arches. He could not foresee his body as another piece of waste floating down in the same obnoxious manner, being found the next day among the plastic bottles, broken down sticks and ill-smelling scum. Juanjo never breathed the excrement, or the bobbing garbage. While the waters swallows his body, the river smells to him of "Oriental Woods." He runs in his home's hallways in his sailor suit, his little patent leather shoes scratching the linoleum floor. When his mother sees him, she tends her arms to receive him. Juanjo holds on to her with all his might, kissing her smiling dimples. He abandons himself to her loving arms, opening his lips to the water of her tenderness. And he listens to Merceditas saying: "How dirty you look, my king!"

Vigo, January 1987